HELP!

Healthy Thinking in Times of Trouble

Gisèle Guénard

iUniverse, Inc.
New York   Bloomington

Help!
Healthy Thinking in Times of Trouble

iUniverse books may be ordered through booksellers or by contacting:

iUniverse
1663 Liberty Drive
Bloomington, IN 47403
www.iuniverse.com
1-800-Authors (1-800-288-4677)

ISBN: 978-1-4502-0208-4 (pbk)
ISBN: 978-1-4502-0210-7 (cloth)
ISBN: 978-1-4502-0209-1 (ebk)

Library of Congress Control Number: 2009914206

Printed in the United States of America

Cover Photography by Nancy Genesse: 4nancy@cyberbeach.net
Images: VisionarEase Inc., Dreamstime, Nancy Genesse

iUniverse rev. date: 2/22/2010

No celebrities or other book authors were interviewed for this publication. The information contained is based on the opinion(s) of the author, at the time of the creation of this work. New information, experiences and emerging research may change or modify this or any person's opinions in the future. This information is not clinical advice. Other persons may have differing opinions. Any products, company names, or/and other commercial terms not owned by the author or by VisionarEase Inc., are used as information for the reader. The author has no known connection to any of these. This book is for information and entertainment, and intended to add to the body of materials in the schools of thought known as healthy and positive thinking. This book is intended to encourage discussion, and to trigger the seeking of professional help, if required by the reader. It is not intended for use as a substitute for medical or business advice or consultation from any licensed health care provider, business consultant or expert in any field. This book does not take the place, of health-care treatment. The reader should consult their health care provider before starting any new health practice.

If for any reason, healthy thinking ideas presented here are contrary to any current healthy thinking strategies the reader is practicing, or contrary to any ideas/ therapy recommended or prescribed by the reader's licensed healthcare provider, (nurse practitioner, physician, psychologist, psychiatrists, etc...) the reader is advised to bring the idea forward to her or his practitioner for discussion.

Note: Persons experiencing mood disorders or other mental health problems usually require varying degrees of assistance from professionals and support groups in strengthening their capacity for healthy thinking, wellness and recovery. This book is for information and discussion only. Should you or your loved one be experiencing mental disturbances or symptoms, psychological changes, social problems, or/and physical signs & symptoms of any health changes, please seek the help of your primary health care provider.

The author and publisher expressly disclaim responsibility for any adverse effects arising from the use or application of any of the information contained in this book.

HELP ! Healthy Thinking in Times of Trouble, is not intended to be a scholarly work. References are organized as "Endnotes. Comments. Resources", simply as a starting point for further exploration.

First Edition

visionarease
positive change leadership & consulting

www.visionarease.com

"To my children

and children's children,

who may remember these troublous times,

when we are gone on new adventure…"

Henry Van Dyke

~~

For Holly, Sarah, Gabriel

and the little ones yet to come.

And for Dad, Mitch, Oncles Léo & Gérard, and

for Rose, who has found the lions now, I am sure….

Acknowledgement

I express my heartfelt appreciation to the following people for their support during the writing of HELP!

~ My loving husband and soul mate John, for his rock-solid belief in me
~ The family, friends, collaborators and clients who shared their stories
~ My professional friends and colleagues, for their support of this project

"Remember... *there is always*
something to look forward to."

Yvonne Guénard 1912-2006

Contents

Preface

As I began work on this book, I wondered if I should don a suit of armor or in some way steel myself against the effects of being mentally immersed in "trouble" ... *maybe call upon an angel...*

I chose to constantly re-Energize my own healthy thinking as I researched and wrote in order to protect myself from the inevitable "bad" feelings which naturally result from applying our energy, attention and focus to troublesome subjects. Have you ever noticed how the more you entertain hurtful, frightening, or negative feelings, the more frequently difficult people and challenging issues are a part of your reality?

Those of you interested in the field of modern positive psychology, or who have explored the work of Dr. Martin Seligman, Catherine Ponder, Dr. Deepak Chopra, Dr. Wayne Dyer, or Eckhart Tolle understand what I mean by the last paragraph. In Attract It. *Beyond* Positive Thinking [1], I offered insight into the importance of applying our efforts to effective, healthy thought habits, solutions, and *feeling good* as much of the time as possible. You will see in "HELP !", that the ability to do so is transformational, especially in times of trouble.

Introduction

Our *truly* hearing the author's message, and our acting on the insights we are offered, is the only way any book can help us in troubled times. You do not need to agree with any particular belief shared by leaders in the positive change movement. What is important is to view trouble from the healthiest perspective possible.

HELP! is not written to convince you of anything, but to support you when you need it most. We live in troubled times, with momentum building for revolutionary change, worldwide. Feeling some sort of inner change, or even a spiritual awakening, as we explore and begin to practice new thinking habits, is common. Simple positive relaxation and visualization, as well as meditation and "letting go" strategies, are becoming more commonplace, regardless of spiritual beliefs, religious practices, or even a lack of faith in a higher power. Contrary to "magical thinking"[2] , time-honoured "secrets" such as those within the philosophies of Zen Buddhism, laughter as healthy thinking and mental reframing are all examples of the spiritual revolution now taking place. The power of the subconscious mind, the law of attraction and the scientifically proven capacity for the human brain to change itself through repeated mental exercise, are all elements of contemporary positive psychology.

HELP ! Is not meant to be a scholarly work, as you will see by the Endnotes, which are in commentary style, and not "strictly APA", the American Psychological Association's method for reference listing, a research standard. However, more and more people are collecting books like these as part of their reference library. Though access to the Internet is a great resource for most of us in the developed world (and hopefully soon worldwide), there is nothing like holding a helpful book in one's hands in times of trouble. Sitting at a computer screen may be the perfect source for answers some of the time, yet, nothing will ever replace a good and useful book. I have a reference library packed with excellent books, some of which are a hundred years old, and within the covers of each, is a treasure trove of inspiration. If you are going to collect something, make it good books.

"Books are friends", my mother used to say… and how right she was. Have you ever had the experience of actively, or perhaps unconsciously, seeking an answer to a question, or a solution to a problem, when you opened a book, and *right there*… at the very page... was your answer? I hope that at some point, this book serves you in just such a moment.

Flipping through chapters is the last thing we need when we are in dire straits, and we need an idea, *now*. With that in mind, the first Section is dedicated to some of my favourite strategies for immediate help. The subsequent chapters are devoted to life crisis events, with specific healthy thinking strategies. Climate change, terrorism and political upheaval, nuclear proliferation and ending world poverty are not addressed as separate topics. This book does not provide all the answers for families struggling with teenaged and young adult children lost to the underworld and to the streets, though you will find many insights of value here. You will find inspirational poems, meditation exercises or inspiring quotations interspersed. These will help you in your contemplation for positive change. Graphics within the book support the ideas presented, and may help nourish your healthy visualization.

Oh… and be ready for the odd chuckle. Thank God for "a bit of a laugh in times of trouble."

We consistently underestimate people's willingness to help us…
by a whopping 50%.[3]

Journal of Personality and Social Psychology

SECTION 1

10 Strategies
for
Healthy Thinking

✦

"Until one is committed, there is hesitancy, the chance to draw back, always ineffectiveness. Concerning all acts of initiative (and creation), there is one elementary truth, the ignorance of which kills countless ideas and splendid plans: that the moment one definitely commits oneself, then providence moves too. A whole stream of events issues from the decision, raising in one's favor all manner of unforeseen incidents, meetings and material assistance, which no man could have dreamt would have come his way."[4]

William Hutchinson Murray

~~~~~~

Trouble has common effects on us all. There are solutions I have found to be highly effective in helping us through those effects, and often triggering solutions to the problem itself. I present eleven of my favorites here for you.

Positive Thinking Alone Will Not Suffice.

How did you feel the last time something bad happened to you, and a well-meaning person tried to make you feel better by suggesting you "think positive?" Regardless of whether the issue is loneliness, grief, being bullied, debt, natural disaster, illness, caregiver burnout, heartbreak, failure, divorce, betrayal, or even being fired... *what if* you could manage any bad situation much better than you normally do?

Let's take a familiar scenario... an exam you prepared diligently for, a job interview, a performance appraisal, a first date, or a party you were giving. For some reason, things turned sour. You got a C on the exam, or did not get the job. Or the performance appraisal went poorly and you are afraid you are being set up for termination. Or perhaps the date was a flop, and now you are thinking, "Single is better." Or perhaps your party was a dismal failure, with no one showing up.

Next, you tell a good friend about the event, and are told, "Just think positive, and it will go better next time."

What are you feeling now?

a. You are grateful for your friend's understanding.
b. You look forward to being able to support your friend, the next time he or she needs you.
c. A basic instinct tells you to express your disappointment and walk away.
d. You feel worse.

Real problems need real solutions. You need more than just inspirational quotes. You need to be able to implement the ideas that ring true for you, and **you need to essentially,**

- **Think**
- **Say**, and
- **Do**

...things differently... differently than how you usually think, speak, and act... differently than any habit which *may* be contributing to the problem, or prolonging your pain.

Contrary to "The Secret"[5], I do not agree that we "attract every single event to us... even the bad". There are many laws and forces at work in the world, within the human psyche, and in the universe itself.

The bottom line, is that especially in crisis, it is help of some kind that you need, not just positive thinking. Even world-class health organizations, such as the Mayo Clinic, are teaching positive thinking[6], yet you must be able to go beyond 'a good attitude' towards literally *changing the way you think.* Words of wisdom need to become more than just motivational. You need to be able to absorb ideas that ring true *for you*, to shift how you think, speak and act. Only then is achievement or a return to a healthier, more peaceful state possible.

If in fact the problem you are facing is of your own doing, then, you have the power to go in another direction, one that is different from what brought you here in the first place.

If it is disaster beyond your control, which you are grappling with, then you need to be able to think, speak and act in the most potentially successful way possible. Period.

What often happens when we attempt to create sustainable positive change in our personal lives? Until we have created, *own* and *use* more effective ways of thinking, we forget what we should think, say and do, to get to where we want to be! We keep repeating old ineffective patterns. If you think it is challenging to stay on track with healthy strategies on a day-to-day basis, how easy do you think it will be when real tragedy strikes?

The following is not an exhaustive list, but a useful one. In tough times, the simpler your *next step* is to access, to understand and to apply, the better your chances of success.

"Notes" space is reserved in selected page areas for you to keep phone numbers of agencies, people and resources in your area, which you may want to jot down, in the event you, your family or group need them urgently.

1. ACCEPT

Nothing is going to make us free, because only the present moment can make us free.

Eckhart Tolle [7]

Without some grasp of Eckhart's profound wisdom, we continue to struggle, much *more than we need to.*

Accepting whatever is going on at the time of our greatest difficulties is *not* what we want to do. Ever. In the chapter on death, I reflect on denial, disbelief or our instinctive desire to reject bad news. We all know that regardless of how bad the news is when we become aware of it, if it is true, then we cannot change it. *It is already in the past.* Rejecting the truth will only delay our ability to help ourselves.

Examples:
- The boy who is frozen, immobile, for one or several seconds as he sees his cell phone slide off the dock
- The unfaithful husband, whose wife has left him for good, who hides the fact from his friends, family, and other potential sources of help for days and even weeks or more
- The woman who learns that her employer is going out of business, avoids sending our resumes, and hopes for a miracle

- The teenage girl who learns her mother is dying of cancer, and avoids seeking help or building her own support system, going about her day to day life with little change to her routine

The healthy thinking scenario for each of these could look like this:

- The boy springs into action, reaching for his cell phone, the instant he sees it beginning to slide off the dock.
- The man whose wife has left him spends the evening talking about his situation with a trusted friend who has always given him good advice. He then seeks out professional help for his personal problems
- The woman who learns that her employer is going out of business updates her resume, starts applying for jobs, and begins plans to open a sideline business, while consciously maintaining an upbeat helpful attitude, until her last day at work.
- The teenage girl who learns her mother is dying of cancer seeks the help of the school guidance counsellor, who makes sure she joins a support group for teens of a dying parent.

No matter how hard it is to do, facing reality is the first and most important step to take in times of trouble. Great leaders are skilled at doing so quickly and helping their followers to do so, while moving forward. Fully accepting a difficult situation *is* living in the present moment. We are not free, while we are struggling to undo what cannot be undone. The freedom we feel once we accept it, and let go of the negative feelings associated with the struggle, is palpable. We sense a new and energizing feeling of being able to move on. We know the initial period will be difficult, and yet we begin to enjoy the knowledge that one day, *this too shall pass.*

Notes:

2. KNOW THAT TROUBLE WILL PASS

There is much more to this concept than meets the eye.

The following inspirational story, which has many parallels to our recent global recession and the resulting hardships for families worldwide, illustrates it beautifully.

In 1900, Ohio saw the birth of Helene Steiner Rice. Born into a hard working immigrant family, she dreamed of political life as a congressional representative one day. Disaster struck when her father died during the Spanish flu epidemic of 1918, which killed over 50 million people[8]. Only a teenager, she became the family breadwinner, a common reality in the day. Working long hours in a lighting factory, she was progressively promoted, finding her niche as an advertising manager and traveling across the US, speaking as an industry expert.

She married a wealthy banker and lived an abundant life. They had a large home and many luxuries. The stock market crashed shortly after their marriage and they lost everything. Once again, finding solutions was her responsibility. Deep in debt, Helen went back to work. She was employed by a greeting card company and one day while she was at work, her husband committed suicide, leaving her a widow at 32. What next?!

She was determined to have a good life, to be happy and successful, regardless of the catastrophes that had befallen her. She became highly skilled at writing verses and inspirational poetry. Her spirit comes through in her well-known poem "This Too Will Pass Away". The gist of it is within this inspirational quote from the verse:

> "For there is no night without dawning
> And I know that my morning is near." [9]

These words embody the spirit of one of the greatest truths guiding healthy thinkers as we navigate through trouble. Living by this philosophy does not necessarily mean we will always react in the perfect way when facing trials and heartbreak. Overall, however, we will fare well indeed.

Notes:

3. DEVELOP OPTIMISM

You would think the value of optimism would be understood by this point in human evolution. Not so... Look around at your family, colleagues and friends. How are things going for them, generally? How many people do you see who are going through life with a pessimistic attitude? Isn't it painful to watch? If this is your reality, *what if* you could gradually transform that way of thinking, that way of being? There is no dark cloud following anybody. Remember:

Simply Thinking Positive Will Not Do It.

We must go *beyond* positive thinking, and apply strategies that *feel* right to us. Being an optimist is much more than positive thought, repeatedly applied. A recent Canadian study suggests that trying to get people to think positive may not help.

Thinking Positive Can Make You Feel Worse!

Canadian researchers asked subjects to repeat, "I am a lovable person," 16 times within four minutes.[10] Participants with already low self-esteem said they felt *worse*. Of course. Positive thinking alone, and affirmations which do *not* feel true, are ineffective in creating positive change within ourselves and in our lives.

This is at the basis of much of the work being done in positive psychology, as what is required for these types of strategies to work is much more than what are called "affirmations." For example, I am five foot two. Now let's imagine I wish I were taller. I can look in the mirror all day long, day after day, and repeat to myself "I am five foot eight". In no way will this change my height, nor will it make me feel any better about myself. Instead, I teach "A-Statements", a term differentiating effective self-talk from ineffective affirmations.[11] Affirmations may be effective once your limiting beliefs have been eliminated and a deep *Knowing* is established. A-Statements are more effective because they *feel true* at the time we say them.

For example, a man with low self-esteem resulting from a poor body image may use A-Statements such as:

- "I know that the exercise I am doing, and the healthy foods I'm eating, are contributing to my health, and helping me more and more every day."
- "I can see myself in the near future, stronger, more fit, and feeling better about my body image. I look forward to buying some new clothes for my healthier body."

Notice how these statements are more realistic, and *are in alignment with what the person is actually doing* (hopefully) to contribute to the positive change? Notice how the A-Statements generally *feel better*, and are more believable to the inner self? Later on, when the person is truly experiencing noticeable success and starting to feel a flow of confidence, then the person may feel that affirmations such as, "I look hot!" are realistic, and believable to their inner self. Only at that time, do affirmations become effective.

When we hear something that we *know* is *not* true, such as an unrealistic affirmation, our skeptical inner self takes over. This is a defense mechanism, inherent within the human psyche, there to protect us. We may even adhere *more* strongly to what we feel or *know* now *is* true. And if that belief is, "I feel lousy about myself," then *that* is what our reality remains. Our trying to convince ourselves otherwise through unrealistic affirmations can certainly make us feel worse. We may have limiting beliefs, which are blocking our success.

Hope

> *"When we have no hope, we do nothing.*
> *When we do nothing, we have no hope."*
> *Jane Goodall.*[12]

How hopeful are you? Hope is simply one of the most powerful tools we have at our disposal during difficulty. Optimism at its best, it is one of humanity's most supportive allies. Avoiding the cultivation of an attitude of hope is simply opportunity lost. Let's look at one of the most important health research projects undertaken in our time.

The Women's Health Initiative[13] followed over 97,000 postmenopausal American women for over eight years. The women in the study answered questionnaires, which indicated whether their nature was optimistic or cynical, even cynically hostile (Yikes!) Here are just a few of the findings. The optimists,

- Had a 9% *lower* chance of developing heart disease
- Had a 14% *lower* chance of dying of *any* cause
- Had a *lower* incidence of high blood pressure and diabetes

As an added feature, the *cynically hostile women were 16% more likely to die.* This finding has been observed where groups of men were studied as well. A study conducted in the Netherlands, with 999 men *and* women, aged 65 to 85 years, reveals similar results. Dr. Erik J. Giltay, of the Delfland Psychiatric Centre noted that those in the most optimistic group were much more likely to live longer than those in the least optimistic group.[14]

Dr. Hilary A. Tindle, a lead author in the Women's Health Initiative report shares,

"Even the most cynical, hostile individual can change, given the right stimulus, and I see this every day." [15] This is powerful information for anyone with a generally negative or even cynical outlook on life, who is effectively attracting many problems, and who currently believes they cannot change.

The Glass

I once knew a man who was a brilliant professional, but who worked through the days with a cynical outlook. The glass was always half-empty. He sneered at attempts to steer discussion towards more positive, solution-oriented perspectives. I recently ran into this fellow, after many years since our last meeting. I was mesmerized by his new persona. No longer cynical, his conversation was interspersed with cheerful commentary. He even looked different. The face that once had,

"I've got one nerve left, and you're stepping on it!" written all over it, was kind and gentle. His entire demeanour had changed. I never did find out what had created this transformation, but this previously cynical individual was clearly a changed person.

There is no darkness

*"To compensate for what we never can have again, we who are
blind make the everlasting most out of what we still have."*

Jacob Twersky

Would it be possible, in 1939, for a blind man to go to college, graduate cum laude, go on to earn in M.A. and a Ph.D., be the captain of the wrestling team, and win a lightweight championship? Jacob Twersky did. After becoming blind at the age of nine, he developed his senses of hearing, smell and touch, to go on about his life with confidence and determination. He became a counsellor for the blind at the Bronx Veteran Hospital, and helped blind soldiers learn that they could perform as well as sighted people, and even get more out of life.

He became a university professor, and went on to inspire others to take the optimistic road, regardless of how daunting were the challenges.

Note: Blindness is our top health fear, according to the Canadian National Institute for the Blind (CNIB)[16].

The following quote from a Jacob Twersky 1948 Readers Digest article encapsulates optimism in action:

*"My joy was almost unbelievable when I came to realize that
from the descriptions of someone beside me I could make
mental pictures that captured the loveliness I had come so close
to losing."* [17]

This optimistic approach has fascinated me in my work with men and women living with blindness, deafness, amputations, and every manner of disease or condition you can think of. In the few people with serious health conditions whom I have worked with, and who steadfastly hung on to a negative or even cynical attitude, their success at managing their health conditions was significantly less than that of the optimists.

How *Do* I Develop Optimism?

Just how *does* one develop optimism? Choosing even just two or three of the following ideas, and *consciously beginning to implement them* in your day-to-day life, will get you started:

- Begin to enjoy the seemingly insignificant positive aspects of your own day-to-day life: the comfort of your own bed, clean hot and cold running water accessible from your own tap, your relationship with a loved one, or that your arms are mobile and strong.

- Avoid comparing yourself to others who you see as more successful, attractive, happy, or whom you think are living a better life.

- Make it a habit to be observant of all the good things that happen to you day-to-day; only waiting three minutes in line, your child thanking you, or more significant events, such as a healthy result on a medical test. You may want to go a step further and write these down.

- Take your focus away from any putdowns. Simply let them go with an "*Oh, well… they must be having a bad day,*" type of thought. As corny as it sounds, this type of thinking is highly protective of your own self-worth.

- Choose a favourite bracelet, watch, or other piece of jewellery, or make one that is hardly noticeable with string and one or two beads. Wear it for 30 days, as a reminder *to replace* negative thoughts and emotions with happier, hopeful ones, *especially* when you don't feel like it. We need reminders, to create significant change to ingrained thinking habits.

The data from 97,000 women and the attitude of people such as Jacob Twersky's cannot be wrong. The next time you face something you wish was not so, re-ignite your optimism, or better yet, start increasing the level of optimism within your approach to life now.

Notes:

4. ACT ON INSPIRATION

We all experience defining moments in life, and some of these come in our darkest hours. Defining moments often manifest as flashes of clear inspiration. Have you ever had an idea in the middle of the night, or first thing in the morning, and you just had to write it down? Or how about when you are driving along in what many consider an almost meditative state, and a thought comes to you, which is the answer to a question you have had for some time? *Insight is knocking at your door.*

The difference between people who live lives that never quite satisfy them at some deep level, and those who live lives of colour, adventure, love, joy and laughter, is the simple decision to act on ideas, and inspiration. It may be wise in fact, to act quickly on inspiration, especially in times of trouble. Malcolm Gladwell, in his book "Blink", puts it this way:

> *"As human beings, we are capable of extraordinary insight*
> *and instinct. Insight is not a light bulb that goes off inside our*
> *heads. It is a flickering candle that can easily be snuffed out."*[18]

How right he is! History and science are filled with examples of great inventions that came about, thanks to someone having a flash of insight and acting upon it, moving on to the invention process. You might remember stories from your school days such as that of Archimedes jumping out of his bath, shouting "Eureka!" having figured out the relationship between the weight of his body and the displacement of water. And then, there was Newton figuring out the law of gravity from an apple falling on his head. In all probability, you have also had ideas that you could have acted upon, with your inaction perhaps regrettable in retrospect. In crisis, ideas that come swiftly and clearly often prove to be the best.

Leaders, you may recognize this concept as a core competency you are continuously developing. In the workplace, we are fortunate to have others with whom we can share our insight, and together as a group, think things through, ultimately developing the best decisions. In personal life, we often do not have this choice and must act individually, for safety in emergencies.

Several years ago, I was driving my teenage daughter to a friend's house one spring evening. There are 300 lakes in our city, and we had had an unusually high amount of rain. Her friend lived quite a way out of the city, in a rural area. The ditches along the dirt road were overflowing with rainwater. We came upon a washout over the road, with runoff water flowing from one side of the road ditch, across to the other side. It was as if a small creek was flowing across the road. I slowed down, but incorrectly judged that it was safe to go across, veering left. In retrospect, I did have a *gut feeling* that I should not do so. I ignored instinct, and steered my vehicle left, as it seemed to me that was the spot with the least water.

This was a gravel road, and as soon as I began to drive through the water, the unstable ground gave way. The vehicle tipped over onto the driver's side, and began to sink down into a deep gully of swiftly flowing spring water. The car came to rest on its side, with my daughter hanging above me, her seat belt holding her against her seat. Behind the steering wheel, I was at the lowest level. Mud and water began flowing into the vehicle. I knew we had to get out, and fast. The best way out was to go up and through the window of the door on the passenger side, which was now the top of the car. I told my daughter to roll down the window and climb out, quickly.

Later that night, a towing company attempted to pull the vehicle out of the gully, but mud had sucked the car in too deep. They sent another rig, a huge boom truck, which was finally able to hoist the vehicle out, skyward. There are two lessons here. First, I ignored the instinct to avoid going through the water on the left, backup, turn around and go home. Secondly, the inspiration to move quickly, and pull ourselves up and out through the side window may have saved us from grim circumstances. [19]

There is inherent danger, in times of crisis, in *not acting on insight*. If we are not confident in our own insights, we can certainly look to others to "bounce ideas off of," looking to them for solutions. In the end, we will do ourselves no good, and will not help ourselves through crisis if we ignore inspiration.

Insight and Spirituality

The concept of insight is a theme in spiritual philosophy, as a guiding force to help us move through life as successfully as possible. It is literally life changing, as stated by Norm Blanchard:

"Insight alone is not enough to improve our situation. Insight must lead to action. What are we going to "do" with this insightful information? *'Until our lives change as a result of what we have learned, insight remains incomplete. The danger of not acting on insight is that it will create a life of dreaming ... not producing any results or "change".* In reality, insights, like our dreams, fade away. This pattern of Behavior is prevalent in our culture. Action is what makes the difference.'" [20]

Blanchard also shares that in his spiritual care work, he has often observed that the results of people's decision to act on, or ignore insight are often predictable.

While studying for a degree in science, I chose as an elective, a course called "The World's Living Religions". One of the subjects of lively discussion was the origin of yoga. Somewhere around 150 B.C. a scholar (or what some historians believe may have been several scholars) named Patanjali developed the practice of yoga based on the Upanishads, a set of mystical writings within Hinduism. The following quote is attributed to Patanjali:

"When you are inspired by some great purpose, some extraordinary project, all your thoughts break their bonds: Your mind transcends limitations, your consciousness expands in every direction, and you find yourself in a new, great, and wonderful world. Dormant forces, faculties and talents become alive, and you discover yourself to be a greater person by far than you ever dreamed yourself to be."[21]

Notes:

5. GO TO THE SOURCE

In terror, rare is the person, regardless of what they say their spiritual beliefs are, who does not reach out in search of help from The Universal Higher Power.

Call it praying, meditation, talking to God, or any other term you like, there is undeniable power in the reconnection with what I will call, for the purposes of this strategy, Source.

Going to the Source can take many forms in people's internal dialogue. Some people will call aloud, or think a specific plea in their mind, often with an image attached to it, at times of great fear. Some think of Buddha, Jesus, St. Theresa, Krishna, Spirit, Yahweh, Allah, Mary, Shangdi, an angel[22] or a loved one who has died, and with whom they feel a special *helping connection*.

I have received help on many occasions from such a plea or prayer. I am grateful to my parents, and to the kind people I knew as a young Catholic, who taught me how to pray... priests and schoolteachers. In some ways, it is the ultimate Energizing strategy. By "Energize", I mean what I consider the second step in the effective application of the law of attraction to any situation, the first being to Decide exactly what it is you *do* want. In the Decide + Energize process, we need to access and *feel* a *Knowing* that help is on the way. The formula for the concept is not 7, or 11 steps. It looks like this[23]:

<u>DECIDE + ENERGIZE</u>
KNOW

In prayer, we Decide exactly what help we need, and keep that desire in mind, while in some way engaging in (Energizing) dialogue with Source...

the spiritual entity, which may or may not carry a visual identity in our mind.

Most people of my generation and older, learned how to reach for help from the Source or pray, through synagogue services, in church or at school, from leaders in their mosque, or other practices and means. Whether you attend organized religious services within an actual building or not, the knowledge that there *is* a Source, and that *we still deserve and can access the Source's help*, remains. We are *a part of* the Universe, which literally means "One Song", and we instinctively know that help and solace is ours when we need it.

But what about the question,

"What do atheists do when they are really in trouble?"

After more than thirty years as a healthcare professional, I can tell you that rare is the deathbed carrying an atheist through to the other side. Conversions to all kinds of spiritual beliefs and religions are seen daily in times of trouble. It is important however, to respect all people's nature, regardless of spiritual beliefs, including that of agnostics or humanists. Humanists value the acknowledgment of human dignity, and our capacity for fulfillment through scientific learning and other human-dependant means. The humanist rejects religion, espousing a philosophical focus on evolution. In times of trouble, those who espouse humanism reach out to friends, family, and community and draw from the goodness of people and the products of healthy human development.

One Song

> *"A human being is a part of the whole, called by us "Universe",*
> *a part limited in time and space."*
> *Albert Einstein*[24]

Honouring and supporting those who are working within the ranks of organized religion, is important if we are to end practices of exclusion, discrimination, greed, abuse and all manner of Behavior, which is not "of Source". I look forward to the day when organized religions march together as one with secular groups, for the good of all, led by women, men, and people of all races and sexual orientation. Imagine the good that can come of this unity in times of real trouble on a global scale…

And when we are all in big trouble, together, does it really matter, what any individual's beliefs are?

But What if I Don't go to Services?

You may be Catholic, as I am, and may attend services sporadically, or on special occasions, and at various churches. The Catholic community will still welcome you in any time of need. This is probably the same for most religions and religious groups whose practices are truly based on the intent to do good.

A Note on Cults: There are many dangerous cults, of course, led by lost souls intent on self-gratification at the expense of the needy, the lonely, the desperate, and unfortunately, those living with mental illness.

If you are approached by such an organization or person, especially if and when you are in despair,

Seek counsel from a known, trusted individual or recognized community non-profit social service group in your area.

Words for Asking

There is mysterious power in groups of people praying, or having a common mental focus on the same request for help. However, whether you are praying 'solo', or in a group, the concepts are the same. Though the following verse is from the Bible, changing the words and names to match your belief system will provide the same support. The Source does not 'care' what name you call it/her/him.

> *God is our refuge and strength, always ready to help in times of trouble. So we will not fear, even if earthquakes come and the mountains crumble into the sea. Let the oceans roar and foam. Let the mountains tremble as the waters surge! ... The Lord almighty is here among us. Psalm 46:1 KJV*

Notes:

6. THINK DIFFERENTLY

Albert Einstein is credited with various forms of the following statement.

"The only way to solve a problem is to
change the thinking that created it."

I am not about to tell you that this thinking habit is easy. When you are in severe pain from an illness, when you are exhausted from an overwhelmed life, when you are desperately trying to save a family member who has lost their way... it will take strength, conviction and a strong desire for a better reality for you to change your thinking habits.

Take heart. I also know that you *are* able to do it, and will be all the stronger once you are through the storm. Let's keep it simple and look at just one strategy to start with.

Stop The Madness!

Start by a few moments of "putting the brakes on", stopping the madness and paying attention, *noticing exactly what you are thinking about*. What kinds of thoughts are you having? Write two or three of your thoughts down if you can. Are you thinking that your situation is hopeless? Are you thinking you are defeated? Are you thinking you will always be in this situation?

Next, make a choice. Choose to *let go* of those thoughts, to push them away repeatedly if you have to… to *stop thinking them.* Instead, *choose one thought*, one possibility for a better outcome, which *feels* good to you now. Tell yourself you want to get out of this situation. Tell yourself you want to be a in a better reality, one that you begin to develop a mental image of. Keep it simple. Stick to one idea at first, one choice, and one decision.

Continue thinking in this manner and you will find that hopeful ideas begin to flow, and that the possibility of success through this situation, or relief from the difficulty, or some sort of better scenario begins to take shape. Continue repeating this thought replacement strategy as much as you need to, to pull yourself into a more creative, effective state of mind.

Music

Music can instantly change your thoughts, feelings and emotions. Uplifting music is what I call Joyful Noise[25]… from the Source itself. When overwhelmed, we tend to forget we have easy access to such an effective tool for wellness. Look at your current music collection, and focus on what 'lifts you up' (that would eliminate death metal). This is also a good time to pull out your old guitar and re-ignite your passion for music.

Notes:

7. APPLYING INTENTION

"The most powerful weapon on earth is

the human soul on fire."

Field Marshal Ferdinand Foch

You will know that you have experienced a breakthrough in your situation, as soon as you begin to experience the undeniably positive feelings of *clearly intending to reach your goal.*

When your soul is on fire for your own good cause, you are unstoppable. This is the difference between the crestfallen, who never get over a crisis, and those who reclaim joy and even abundance.

Intention is *not* a decision. It is:

- The ongoing honouring of a decision we have made.
- Moving forward, in alignment with an original decision. This includes maintaining thought habits, vocabulary and conversation in line with that decision. Most importantly, it includes taking *only* actions that are aligned with that decision.
- The application of creativity in alignment with our original decision.

- Unwavering in its 'match' to our accessing all that is good for us in this life

Peace After Trauma

As a little girl, I remember being afraid to go to the funeral home for a relative's wake, and my mother telling me, in a kind and teaching way,

"It's not the dead you need to be afraid of, child. It's the living."

Only those who have experienced it, and their families, can truly understand the nightmare of child abduction.

As a testament to the power of intention, few stories match that of Elizabeth Smart. Kidnapped by a convicted sex offender and held for nine months, she managed to escape and was reunited with her family. During interviews after the nightmare, she frequently relates that her mother's words helped her tremendously.

"They already took nine months of your life away. Don't give them anymore,"

she quotes her mother as saying.

"So I just didn't think about being sad, because I was so happy to be home, and when my mom said that to me, I thought about it and tried to carry that out the rest of my life because I think that really is true. I think if a person dwells upon something for so long, it will control them and it's harder for someone to move on with that."[26]

Elizabeth's words were wise far beyond her years.

We, as a caring society, must do everything we possibly can to ensure the protection of our children. We must put an end to child abduction.

You Do What You Have to Do

Or how about the story of Aaron Ralston, who found himself trapped under a boulder in Utah's Canyons. After four days, realizing no one was coming to his rescue, he had no intention of dying there. Using his pocketknife, he cut off his arm, applied a tourniquet, and made it to safety.[27] He is still climbing mountains. Intention is a powerful thing indeed.

Though no one in his or her right mind advocates self-amputation, or self-mutilation of any kind, we do not know what choices we would be required to make in order to save our own life, or the life of a loved one.

Notes:

8. THE POWER OF THANKS

And then there is gratitude.

It is sometimes painfully difficult for us to express gratitude when something bad has happened to us. The worse the event is, the less we may feel the natural instinct to be grateful for what we do have. Take a closer look however, at the habits of people who seem to get through all manner of problems and still be happy. I have had the pleasure of meeting people who are enjoying life and thankful for the experiences they *are* able to have, even after terminal diagnosis, losing a home, bankruptcy, the loss of a loved one, academic failure and betrayal, just to name a few.

What is the point of making ourselves feel worse by wallowing in it, and applying our attention, energy and focus to the horrible hand we have been dealt? Find a way to remind yourself, especially in difficult times: one of your main goals is to seek out ways to trigger or generate good feelings within yourself.

Don't Knock It 'Til You've Tried It

Why is an attitude of gratefulness a common thread in the new positive psychology, and all successful self-help systems? *Because it works.* Consciously applying gratitude strategies helps us to refocus on what *is* working in our life, generates hopeful feelings about ourselves and the potential of our situation, and may even help us find solutions.

How do we do this? The simple answer is to develop the *daily* practice of observing and acknowledging any good within your life. And unless you have already passed on to the other side, there is always something to be grateful for, even if it is the breath you take. People facing death often express gratefulness about the life they have enjoyed, and that they will soon be free of pain and suffering.

Journaling, making short lists on a daily basis, or simply making a point of thinking about all the things you have to be grateful for, are easy strategies. As a mental practice before going to bed at night and as a 'first thing in the morning' exercise, the habit is easier to develop. Try the Bedtime Meditation exercise at the end of this section, the next time you cannot sleep in the middle of the night.

Note about journaling: relax about it. Do not become a slave to it or feel guilty if you are not writing in your journal as often as you had originally planned. It should be an enjoyable uplifting experience, and should generate good feelings within you. If you don't feel like it, wait until you do. Become obsessive about it when it does not feel good, makes journaling counter productive.

On the following page is a Bedtime Meditation which is also a gratitude strategy, helping us to re-focus on the positive aspects of our lives. In times of crisis, this is a powerful exercise. It will help take your mind off the most difficult aspects of a problem, as well as help you focus on something that actually makes you feel good.

In the worst of catastrophes, if you are still breathing and conscious, there is always a way to express gratitude. I learned about gratitude from a master. When my mother was dying, at the age of 94, weighing about 60 pounds, blind and struggling, as I was leaving her bedside I would always say to her,

"Mom I'll be back tonight," or whatever the plan was. She would always brighten up and respond,

"Oh good! Something to look forward to."

Bedtime Meditation

1. Empty your bladder and get comfortable. Find your favorite sleeping position.

2. Take two or three relaxing deep breaths, making sure your belly rises as you breathe in, and breathing out through your lungs thoroughly and slowly.

3. Now mentally go through the alphabet, and think of one element of your life you are grateful for, as you think of each letter. For example, a person you love whose name starts with "A"; and then for "B", a banana you enjoyed, followed by the coaching you liked for "C", and so on. In all probability, you will not get much further than the letter L.

Notes:

9. CREATE

You have genius within you, and you can use your creative abilities to help yourself through any situation.

"If you've been taught to avoid thinking too highly of yourself, and that genius is reserved for a handful of select individuals, you probably accepted the idea. You won't recognize your genius aspect if you've been conditioned to believe that you should accept your lot in life, think small, try to fit in with normal groups of people, and not aim too high in order to avoid disappointment." [28] Dr. Wayne Dyer

Many of the world's greatest inventions and innovations came about in times of crisis. You can apply the same principle on an individual level at any time. Have you ever had the experience of being ill for a period, perhaps hospitalized, or at home recuperating? And during that period, have you had the experience of feeling a surge of desire to do/learn/experience/change and create, as soon as you were well? Or perhaps you have been drawn to act in the service of others in times of crisis? You are not alone:

- John Stetson, who invented the Stetson cowboy hat after having developed tuberculosis, moved west to improve his health and saw an opportunity in combining his skills with the needs of the cowboy. [29]
- Blood supply was critically low as war tore across Europe in 1940. Dr. Charles Drew was appointed by international leaders to find

a solution. He led the collection, processing and transportation of over 14,000 units of plasma - in less than five months. His research helped revolutionize blood plasma transfusion for the battlefield, saving thousands of lives and providing a platform for modern hematology.[30]

In both of these examples, creativity in times of trouble... *thinking differently* than everyone else, is at the core of the solutions found. If you ignore the fear and doubt, which may be present when you receive a flash of creative insight at times like these, you will be amazed at the solutions, which will reveal themselves. The impetus for the start of many successful businesses is *crisis*.

Turning Crisis Into Opportunity ™ [31] is exactly what countless women, men and groups have done, changing their lot in life *dramatically* at the worst possible time. During this past recession, thousands of people opened new businesses, saying losing their job was one of the best things that have happened to them[32].

Note: A study published, conducted by biofeedback expert, Dr. Robert H. Reiner showed that women engaged in creative activities such as painting and sewing had measurable positive health changes.[33]

The Long Walk to Freedom

Imprisoned from 1964 to 1990, Nelson Mandela, driven to continue his life's work and service to his people, exercised his creativity *while in prison*. He was determined to write his autobiography, knowing of the millions who depended on him as their leader, and the historically inspirational value of such a work. He was required to write in secret, with his manuscript eventually discovered by authorities and confiscated. Co-prisoners had miraculously insured that the original manuscript was saved.[34]

Here are a few ways to trigger and boost your own creativity when times are tough:

- Do a quick self-check, to determine if you are in panic mode. If you are walking about aimlessly, breathing with shallow breaths, and have a feeling that you are running around in circles, you need to get a grip. Stop and do some simple deep breathing. Really. Three or four deep breaths may be all you need to regain your balance. You will only be able to access your creative nature once you are back on solid mental and emotional ground.

- Spend time in nature, or the most beautiful surrounding you can access at the time, to help clear your mind and reconnect with all that is good. If it is not possible for you to do so, close your eyes and work on creating the clearest nature visual that you can, exactly as you would love to experience it.

- Pay attention to whatever activity draws you to it, the activity that causes you to lose track of time. For some people this is the type of work we love doing, regardless of monetary gain. This natural penchant for a particular activity often points to a wise choice for those seeking to diversify their income with sideline businesses, or develop new businesses after financial crisis.

- Avoid giving your attention, energy and focus to bad news. When reading the newspaper, scan the bad news headlines quickly and read at greater length, the articles with a positive focus. Spend a few moments watching important news stories, unless they are solution oriented.

- Now begin some solitary or group brainstorming to come up with ideas as the basis for solutions to your problem.

Notes:

10. USE HUMOR

Life does not cease to be funny when someone dies,
anymore than it ceases to be serious when someone laughs.

George Bernard Shaw

Should we avoid using humor in times of trouble? To the contrary. It is precisely what we need, in a manner, and as soon as it is *appropriate.* It takes some skill, natural insight, or study of

how to best inject humor when the time is right. Yet correctly injected, a good laugh changes everything. It gives a perspective and welcomed relief. I have even seen it contribute significantly to team alignment in times of big trouble.

It's a Funeral. No Laughing, Please.

The ability to laugh at ourselves is a gift we should use more often. How many of us have had the strange and delightful experience of a good belly laugh at the funeral of a loved one? You know, that moment where you go from crying your eyes out, to laughing in the coffee room? Didn't that feel great? I hope any memorial service in my honour is a joyous affair with lots of laughs, merriment and general gaiety. (Go for it, friends... I'll be there with you!)

There is a time for everything, and there are moments during crisis where it is absolutely *not* appropriate to pursue any attempt at humor. Some have learned this the hard way. Whenever I am asked to do a eulogy however, if possible, I make sure to include at least one respectful anecdote that will get a laugh from the grieving crowd. It is not only a relief but it is also showing respect and honouring the good times that the deceased enjoyed.

A Delicate Balance

Dr. Stephen M. Sultanoff, an expert in therapeutic humor cautions, "However, during a crisis humor is often experienced and perceived by individuals immersed in the crisis as insensitive and even hurtful."[35] Being sensitive to pain experienced by others is required before and during the use of humor in bad situations. If you have no relationship with the people experiencing a crisis, you are probably not the person who should attempt to get them laughing. On several occasions, I have been fascinated to observe the well meaning, yet sadly misguided, attempts at excessive cheerfulness by individuals hired to provide spiritual care services within healthcare organizations.

When we are close to the situation, we may not think something is humorous in the least. Later on however, we may be laughing aloud about some ridiculous moment that occurred during a crisis. Here is one my family experienced during the last moments of my father's life.

My Dad was diagnosed with atherosclerosis (life-threatening plaque buildup in the arteries) and subsequently had quadruple bypass surgery. The day after the operation, the cardiac surgeons told us that the results were not good. Deadly plaque was already starting to block the new arteries feeding his heart. We were told he had a year at best.

He recuperated from the surgery, only to suffer a stroke about two years later. Determined, he followed his rehabilitation program and was managing well, when he suffered a fatal heart attack. He was only 61, and after several attempts at resuscitation by ER and ICU staff, we were asked if we would agree to the removing life support. Knowing it was hopeless, we made the painful decision and asked that a priest come in to deliver the Sacrament of the sick.

None of us had ever met this priest before, and as he stood near the head of the bed, with all of us tearfully gathered round, a breathing tube providing oxygen for my dying father, the priest began to flip the pages of his prayer book back and forth, over and over. He became flustered, red-faced and yet seemed quite determined to find exactly what he was looking for. And then it all became clear. You see, this is the year that Pope John Paul II was coming to Canada. And our priest was determined to use some special prayer that linked the pope's visit to my father's dying. Somehow, he was convinced this is exactly what we all needed, and most certainly, what my father needed.

Anyone who knew my father, would have known that, had he any awareness of this bizarre event, he would have wanted the Priest to, "Just get on with it, please!" He finally found what he was looking for, we all suffered through the Pope-focused prayer, and enjoyed a good laugh about it later on. The hilarity of this well-meaning man of God being convinced that the priority issue was the Pope's Canada visit, during my father's last moments, was quite entertaining and still is.

Note: I share this story with all due respect to Pope John Paul II who was a wonderful man, for whom my family and I had great respect. In fact, my younger brother was one of the youth Corps who participated in serving at the time of the pontiff's visit in Ottawa.

Get Your Own

Using all resources at your disposal during times of trouble is wise. Humor is one of them. You may not feel responsible for cheering anyone else up, yet it would be wise to develop habits or prepare yourself to be able to access your own funny bone when you need it.

What does your collection of movies look like? Drama, violence, horrors, pornography and death? Or do you have a number of comedies guaranteed to make you smile or maybe even laugh? Do you have a few joke books lying around? Have you bookmarked some hilarious Internet sites? If not, now's the time. It is a great idea as a general life habit, to laugh out loud at least three times a day, in my experience. Here are just a few reasons why:

A. Laughter is contagious. If you do not believe me, or you have not seen this team activity in action, simply start laughing out loud, even if you don't feel like it. Keep going until, guess what... you actually start laughing for real, at the ridiculousness of it. For speedier results, do it in front of the mirror. Laughter therapy is gaining popularity, and you can probably find a laughter workshop in a city near you. In other words, your laughter may be "caught" by others in your vicinity, triggering good feelings amongst all, when everybody needs it most.

B. Shared laughter binds people together, as I mentioned earlier, and helps with team alignment. I recommend to my management clients that, unless inappropriate, they open staff meetings with something lighthearted, or outright funny. Start this trend at work: people will look forward to staff meetings to see what you come up with next.

C. You have heard of the resulting endorphin release from laughter. Numerous studies have supported scientific findings that laughter can strengthen your immune system, help decrease pain, increase your energy, and protect you from the dangerous effects of stress.[36]

Even geniuses appreciate laughter.

"If we knew what it was we were doing, it would not be called research, would it?" Albert Einstein

Notes:

CONTRIBUTE TO THE POSITIVE CHANGE MOVEMENT

We are at the edge of the abyss. Thankfully, more and more people of all ages are joining, in what is nothing less than a revolution of the spirit. Out of adversity, or out of a drive to be an agent for positive change, there is a tidal wave of efforts towards the liberation of the oppressed and the saving of our planet.

Spectacular advancements in the ease of information transfer online have opened a window into atrocities being carried out, which we would not have known of in the past. Ultimately, as always happens eventually, the forces of good are rallying. There are organizations, new and old, meeting the call to help the weak, the vulnerable, the illiterate, and the abused.

The positive change movement is the most important effort at work in the world today. It has many faces, as is required. It has the potential to positively affect any issue, minor and major, facing every one of us. In the professional world, in organizations, government initiatives and in small groups as well as with individuals, there is a powerful and renewed focus on applying knowledge, resources and positive strategies to effect change.

Conscious leadership, conscious capitalism, spirituality at work ... these are all part of the culture shift we are experiencing. As Patricia Aberdeen so clearly states in Megatrends 2010 - this is the biggest shift since the information age.[37] The most recent evidence of the shift was of course the economic crisis of 2008-2009. Your individual actions in times of trouble and in any leadership role you play, can contribute to the impact of the positive change movement. Let's look at the following stories highlighting the movement we know is the answer to our most destructive problems.

A Voice for Abducted Children.

I bring back Elizabeth Smart for this poignant story. After her rescue following her abduction, Elizabeth Smart decided to put her traumatic experience to work to help others. In partnership with the US Department of Justice and for other children who survived an abduction, she has co-authored a powerful and practical book for victims. It is written by children, now teenagers and adults, in the abducted child's voice, in their language, with strategies and suggestions for prevention. Entitled,

"You're Not Alone.
The Journey From Abduction to Empowerment."

It is a moving example of doing good with what you know.[38] The book is intended for those who have suffered through abduction. However, its content is a powerful tool for prevention, and Elizabeth has been quoted as saying she wants everyone to read the book.[39] I highly recommend it and it is available free of charge as a PDF online. The link is in the Endnotes.

The creation of the book came about through an invitation by the U. S.

government, to the survivors, to participate in sharing their stories. It tells the true account of five young people who were abducted in differing situations. The book also lists resources you can use if you have been abducted and need to talk to someone or obtain therapy. Included is a list of everyday activities to help a victim integrate back into their former lives. There are tips for overcoming guilt and different ways to look at one's own situation, many of which are embedded in the riveting stories the authors tell.

Cancer Diagnosis Triggers Woman's Mission.

So far, there are no millionaire philanthropists or major grants, for Dana Dornsife's new nonprofit organization, the Lazarex Cancer Foundation. After her beloved brother-in-law was diagnosed with cancer of the pancreas, Dana founded the LCF to help bring hope, dignity and a better life for cancer patients and those who love them. Since 2006, Dana and the LCF have been hosting major events such as marathons, rock concerts and Halloween parties. Specifically, the LCF is helping patients financially through clinical trials, flying them to the location of the trials and even paying for their apartment or their gas. They are dealing with end stage patients, those who cannot wait for a cure. Susan Sappington, Lazarex Director of Development says,

"You're not going to save everyone. There are many many patients who pass on. Sometimes I think, 'Why are we doing this?' Then we get letters from families thanking us. That is why this is important to us. I wake up every morning knowing that I'm doing something for somebody and changing the world. I truly believe that."[40]

From Victim to Survivor to Active Citizen.

The faster women and girls gain equal rights, freedom and safety, the faster planet earth will heal. Please share this message.

At the age of 11, Zainab Salbi's father was forced to become Saddam

Hussein's personal pilot. Often made to be part of the Hussein household, Zainab's mother, in an attempt at protecting her child, sent her into an arranged marriage in the US. It turned out to be a nightmare. She developed a new identity as a crusader for women survivors of war and founded Women for Women International.

"For very good reasons, I have come to trust no one, not even my mother. I had just turned 21, and I found myself all alone for the first time as fresh new fears were steeped on all the old ones. I did what I needed to survive, though it was not nearly as simple as I make it sound: I erased the pilot's daughter and started over." Zainab Salbi [41]

Zainab Salbi's organization, Women for Women International, helps women who have been tortured and abused, and who have suffered female genital mutilation, (FGM)[42]. Working wherever the need is greatest, they are in countries such as Afghanistan, Iraq, and Rwanda. Through their efforts, women are mobilized to transform their lives with a holistic approach that addresses the unique needs of each woman. They work with women who may have lost all that they had, including their dignity and their health. These are women in conflict and who have nowhere else to turn. Women enter programs and begin a journey from victim to survivor to active citizen.

The Green Revolution for Peace:

> *"More than any other single person of his age, he has helped to provide bread for a hungry world. We have made this choice in the hope that providing bread will also give the world peace."*
>
> *Nobel Peace Prize committee chairman Aase Lionaes, presenting the award to Dr. Norman Borlaug.* [43]

Born on an Iowa family farm, and deeply marked by the Great Depression and its effect on families undernourished and destitute, Dr. Norman Borlaug spent much of his life as an activist against famine. He was quoted as saying,

"You'd see young people asking for a nickel to buy bread and older people sleeping in the park," he said. "We were a pretty sick nation at that time. It made me tough. I was angry that this kind of condition could exist and persist in our own society."

As soon as he could, after the Second World War, Norman joined a program to help Mexican farmers struggling in poverty. As part of a team, he developed higher-yielding, adaptable disease resistant wheat.

In the 1960s, famine was looming in India and Pakistan. The voices of doom were predicting mass starvation. Knowing his new wheat seeds could avert disaster, bureaucrats, who at first turned him away, permitted him to move ahead with his ideas.

India and Pakistan became self-sufficient in wheat production within eight years. In his Nobel Prize acceptance speech, Dr. Borlaug quoted the prize's creator, Alfred Nobel:

"I would rather take care of the stomachs of the living than the glory of the departed in the form of monuments." [44]

"Did I pass?" The Nurse Practitioner Solution.

Theresa (not her real name) sat in the examination room, nervously wondering if once again, she would be unable to find anyone to take care of her in her old age. A "typical" senior citizen, white hair, unassuming, she hoped to manage well with her health issues, and enjoy this part of her life. She had just finished nervously answering the health history questions Marilyn, the Nurse Practitioner, carefully asked her, as part of the initial assessment. As it dawned on Marilyn that this woman thought she had to "pass" certain criteria in order to be accepted into the healthcare practice of the brand-new clinic, the magnitude of the impact their little clinic was having on people's lives dawned on her.

Having been an orphan patient for years, accessing essential health care only through walk-in clinics and emergency departments, Theresa was among the 5 million Canadians without access to primary health care, which has traditionally been provided by family physicians. Even with the development of Family Health Teams (FHT) in Ontario, such as the model Espanola and Area Family Health Team[45], many nurse practitioners graduating in Ontario were unable to find full-time employment under their current scope of practice.

Marilyn Butcher, Roberta Heale and their team decided to break down barriers, and do something to help the thousands of people in their community who now found themselves orphan patients. They made the decision to think, speak and act differently.

Though it had never been done before, and many said it could not be done, they and their team forged ahead, sacrificing much, and battling many startup issues. With the support of the government of Ontario, they opened the first nurse practitioner-led primary health care clinic in Canada. "The day we opened our doors to start registering people," says Butcher, "there was a sea of gray hair in the parking lot, many of them using walkers and canes." Within a short period, their tiny clinic was providing health care for over 2000 patients, many of them with complex healthcare conditions that regularly triggered visits to emergency department care.

Today, the Ontario Ministry of Health and Long Term Care,[46] nurse practitioners, physicians, social workers, physiotherapists, dietitians, nurses, and other health care professionals are collaborating to open 25 nurse practitioner-led clinics in Ontario. The Sudbury District Nurse Practitioner Clinic[47] is now a model for a movement that is making a difference in thousands of peoples' lives. The NP-led clinics and the FHT strategy are key elements in the solution to our looming health-care crisis.

The Power of Children

Children want to, and can, participate in global events that are meaningful to them. Their efforts are now proving to be powerful in positively affecting world issues. Take the astonishing success of Free the Children.[48]

The mission of the organization, founded by Craig Kielburger in 1995 *at the age of 12* is:

- To free children from poverty and exploitation
- To free young people from the notion that they are powerless to affect positive change in the world.

Through education, it is now the world's largest network of children helping children. Over one million are involved in the unique programs, in 45 countries. To date, the organization has won:

- The World's Children's Prize for the Rights of the Child
- The Human Rights Award from the World Association of Non-Governmental Organizations.

Free The Children has also formed successful partnerships with leading school boards and Oprah's Angel Network.[49] These are children thinking effectively, communicating for change, and acting to literally, save the world.

Tipping Point

We come from a time when the limits of our capacity for information transfer, and the obstacles of distance and geography enabled a limited number of charitable organizations to exist and flourish. This millennium is changing all that. We are reaching a tipping point in the number of people actively working in the positive change movement.

I defer to Malcolm Gladwell, who coined the phrase in his brilliant work. "The Tipping Point. How Little Things Can Make the Difference."

"The tipping point is the biography of an idea, and the idea is very simple. It is that the best way to understand the emergence of fashion trends, the ebb and flow of crime waves, or, for that matter, the transformation of unknown books into bestsellers, or the rise of teenage smoking, or the phenomena of word-of-mouth, or any member of the other mysterious changes that mark everyday life is to think of them as epidemics. Ideas and products and messages and behaviors spread just like viruses do." Malcolm Gladwell[50]

What if together, we can
turn the positive change movement into a pandemic?

Notes:

SECTION 2

Help for the Human Journey

✦

Chapter 1

Mental Health Challenges

1. Bring support.

2. Remember to breathe.

3. Find a health advocate.

4. Get a second opinion.

5. Become an expert on your illness.

Dr. Mehmet Oz. His top five strategies
for when you are diagnosed with serious illness.[51]

The Miracle of Mental Wellness

Have you ever witnessed the miracle of wellness emerge in a person who has
suffered from mental illness? Have you been fortunate enough to experience

this miracle yourself? Do you believe it is possible for someone who suffers a severe depression to come through it, rise up, and never suffer another episode? What if there were simple, zero cost personal strategies available to any of us that were often capable of preventing our slide into deeper and deeper melancholy? And what if, for most of us, those exact strategies were effective in day-to-day life, most, or all of the time?

It is a testament to the resilience of the human mind, and to the healing power of the love of family and friends, that the number of people suffering from mental illness is as low as it is. People have lived through tremendous personal pain and even what some would consider catastrophe, and yet are well and enjoying life today. They have achieved many of their personal goals, and are having great relationships. What differentiates these people from those who cannot find their way out of depression or the most preventable of mental illness, such as addiction?

I am not an expert in mental health care, though I will share with you, that during my nursing career, I did work in a large, and in a midsize mental institution, as well as on patient care units in a general hospital for those suffering mental health illness. I also developed curriculum and taught mental health courses to hundreds of nursing students. I have a deep feeling of empathy for those among us who suffer the ravages of mental illness. It has touched my family deeply, with my beautiful brother Mitch dying at 41, in a drug and alcohol-related motorcycle accident. It has always been the dark side of the human condition, and always will be. It is a factor, or a result, of much human suffering, including addiction, crime, sexual abuse, and political turmoil at the hands of those delusional and obsessed with greed and lust for power.

In reading this chapter, keep in mind...

Unhappiness is Not an Illness

With 24/7 media bombardment telling us we need to be super happy, super beautiful, super successful and super young all the time, keep in mind, that being unhappy some of the time is not an illness. It is normal. No one needs to seek therapy, treatment or any other sort of relief for occasional periods of unhappiness. I suggest that it is quite normal for all of us to have some unhappiness on a daily basis, sometimes for a few minutes, sometimes longer. It is not pathological to experience this normal part of the human condition. The only people whom I have known, who were experiencing constant happiness, for the entire period of time in which I was part of their life, were in fact experiencing serious mental illness.

My favorite red flag about our culture's obsession with constant happiness is the classification of severe premenstrual symptoms as a psychiatric disorder in the DSM. (!) The title given is Premenstrual Dysphoric Disorder, PMDD. The DSM is the worldwide Encyclopedia, the gold standard, the Bible for diagnosis of mental illness by health care professionals. Somehow, in the last century, this "level" of premenstrual syndrome was successfully entered into the DSM (Diagnostic and Statistical Manual of Mental Disorders), with this new classification remaining controversial today. Experts in the field are continuing efforts to have it removed from the DSM, including the feisty Dr. Paula J. Caplan[52]. For some enlightening and somewhat philosophical study on the matter, you will enjoy Mark Kingwell's national bestseller, "Better Living. In Pursuit of Happiness from Plato to Prozac" and in particular, his section "So Happy It's Nuts!"[53]

Advancements and Discoveries

Since 1974, when I was introduced to my first patient suffering with schizophrenia, the advances in care and wellness for mental health conditions is encouraging to say the least. He was 24, attractive and highly intelligent. I was a teen-aged nursing student at a behemoth sized psychiatric institution. This was before the de-institutionalization of the mentally ill. This was before the streets of our big cities were "home" to 100's of thousands of lost souls, unable to cope without the caring support of in-house care.

My patient was trying to teach me to play chess… I still remember his face. I got a call from my clinical instructor one Saturday morning. He had gone out on a weekend pass, and lied down across the train tracks. His suicide was shocking to me… yet not unexpected, to his circle of caregivers, family and friends.

Though the risk of suicide is still 50 times higher for people living with schizophrenia than in the general population, with 40% attempting it at least once, there is reason for hope. [54] Optimism for people living with mental illness and for those of you who have loved ones living with it is well founded. Review with me the following facts.

Real Hope

1. **The brain can *repair and change itself*, through healthy thinking and the repetitive use of new habits.**

The brain is capable of repairing its own nerve cell damage and can even develop new nerve cells, or neurons.[55] An agent has been found at work within the human brain, triggering this startling phenomenon. This agent is called Brain Derived Neurotropic Factor, or BDNF. Amazing results have been seen in children and adults, even with catastrophic conditions such a post hemispherectomy (the removal of one side of the brain)[56], after massive stroke, and even in blindness and other previously hopeless conditions. A great deal of research is being done in this area, in the quest for ongoing breakthroughs in the treatment of depression and other conditions. More about this later, under 'Brain Plasticity'.

2.   Exercise: Major Relief for Depression.

Have you ever been inactive for a period, and then began to exercise daily again? How did you feel mentally, emotionally? Remarkable positive chemical and physiological changes occur in our brain, and our entire central nervous system with exercise. Exercise may work on improving mood by altering the circulation of serotonin, norepinephrine, and the endorphins flowing through our bodies and brain cells. Not only does exercise help lift our mood when we are depressed, studies show that it can help prevent relapse, and for many, may be as effective as anti-depressant medication. Psychiatrist Dr. James Gordon, founder of the Center for Mind-Body Medicine in Washington, D.C., explains why.

"'Do we really need Prozac?' he asks. There is a better way to treat depression— through diet, exercise and meditation. Roll your eyes all you like. He's used the approach for 35 years with a wide range of patients, from runaway children and middle-class adults in Washington, D.C., to victims of war in Bosnia, Kosovo, Israel and the Gaza Strip."[57]

3.   The discovery and development of antipsychotic drugs for the treatment of schizophrenia. [58]

Prior to the discovery of antipsychotic drugs, people and families affected by schizophrenia faced a gloomy and often terrifying day-to-day existence. Though all of us would prefer to live a medication-free life, those of you who live with schizophrenia know the great benefit you experience through compliance with a successful medication treatment plan. There is every reason to believe that significant advancement in the treatment of schizophrenia is inevitable. The possibility of a better life in the future for people who have schizophrenia is growing significantly. In 2003 Dr. Thomas Insel, as Director of the U.S. National Institute for Mental Health (NIMH) has stated that with the right investments, *scientists are within reach of finding a cure for schizophrenia in the next ten years.* [59]

4. **Protein masses found in the brains of people with Alzheimer's disease destroy brain cells.**[60]

A chemical called ganglioside GM-1 and cholesterol are both linked in some way to these protein masses. These discoveries are the basis for further research towards the development of memory restoring and memory promoting drugs. It is realistic to look forward to an effective treatment for Alzheimer's *early in this century.*

5. **More new non-drug treatments for serious mental illness such as of schizophrenia are in development.**[61]

Many new psychosocial therapies are also in development, some being used with significant success. One of these is CBT, or Cognitive Behavioral Therapy, which helps the patient to *re-direct his or her thoughts towards more positive ideation*, Behavior and emotions. CBT is delivered by trained mental health care professionals.

I share these advancements, as there is absolutely no doubt that science will continue to make magnificent, life-changing discoveries. There was a time when people lived and died in an iron lung, when diabetes and breast cancer were death sentences, and when smallpox killed over 300 million people in the 20th century. Just as smallpox was eradicated in 1979, other diseases will fall in time[62]. There are dedicated, caring, committed researchers working in laboratories, in research studies, in hospitals and community clinics all over the world, on these illnesses and conditions. Many of these people have had personal experience with mental illness or members of their families. They are driven. Their patients, friends or loved ones struggle with mental illness, and these people, these brilliant minds think differently. They care deeply about finding treatments and cures for mental illness. There is reason for hope, and there is reason for optimism.

Family History

Have you ever thought about sharing information from your history about those family members who have had mental illness, with your nurse or your physician? There are many unwritten taboos and issues of stigma, or labeling, around mental illness. One of the family history facts that we tend to avoid mentioning during any health care event, is that someone in our family may have had one or more episodes of mental illness. We are uncomfortable about this. We prefer to forget about it. Or, we may believe that it is of no importance to our own health. On the contrary, this information may help your primary care provider fully assess, and perhaps even help prevent, health issues you may have now or in the future.

Researchers are masters at healthy thinking: they ask the trigger question Einstein used incessantly, *"What If?"*

A large and distinguished group of researchers recently studied the "family/mental illness correlation" issue in New Zealand. Their findings suggest that the sharing of family history around mental health issues is of key significance in predicting the severity of mental disease for patients.[63] Their research strongly suggests that a person's risk for developing depression, anxiety, addiction and even how serious that future illness might be, can be accurately predicted *with 30 minutes or less* of assessment about the patient's family history.

Think about, and plan your next health care visit. Plan to tell your primary care provider, about any mental illness present or past, in your family. Be open to discussing any possible areas of concern around your own mental health with your care provider.

Want to Lower Your Chances of Developing Schizophrenia?

Better your odds... don't start using. Dozens of research studies show that using pot (marijuana, cannabis, weed, grass, hashish, hash, hash oil) and other street drugs increase your chance of developing depression or schizophrenia... *dramatically*. Plus, you have no way of knowing what has been added to a street drug. Research suggests that avoiding use of all street drugs could greatly reduce your chance (by as much as 50% to 80% if you are biologically predisposed) of developing schizophrenia. Abstaining from marijuana use *after* developing schizophrenia also helps reduce relapse rates.

Do you have any family member with a history of mental illness? Do not use even small amounts of cannabis, if you have had an episode of paranoid thinking, hearing voices or had a bad response when first trying cannabis or, using a small amount. Other street drugs are also extremely dangerous. This is in part due to their being produced in home laboratories with virtually any possible combination of additional substances mixed in with the drugs." [64]

Seeking Treatment

From anorexia to addiction and depression, within my own circle of family, friends and acquaintances, there has been more than one tragic, and many near tragic events related to mental health problems. Fortunately, most of these people sought treatment or were assisted to seek treatment by those who cared for them. For a few, this treatment included in-patient care on a mental health unit. For those of us who were involved in the lives of these people during those times of crisis, we no longer see the possibility of being in a mental health hospital bed as something "out there", something only others, far removed from "us", would experience. We now know that the saying "There, but for the grace of God go I," is based in absolute truth. Any of us could experience the need for mental health treatment, and fortunately, for the most part, healthcare systems in the developed world do provide a safety net. I hope that all nations will one day have such resources for all people.

How do I know if I need treatment?

The number one safety valve for any of us whose mental status may not be 100% healthy at any given time, is to know the answer to the above question. Countless lives have been saved by the person experiencing mental illness reaching out, and saying to somebody, "**I need help.**"

Physicians, nurse practitioners, psychiatrists and psychologists use specific assessment tools to diagnose mental illness, such as the following questions:

- Has your behavior changed recently?
- Have you, your family members or your friends noticed that you are acting differently?
- Do you find that your level of anxiety and stress has increased and is becoming difficult to tolerate?
- Are you falling into a pattern of substance abuse?
- Have your sleeping and eating habits changed?

Answering these questions frankly will help you, your health care providers and your caregivers determine if you need help. Different conditions and illnesses present different signs and symptoms. Do you know whether you or someone you know is suicidal or nearing a suicidal state of mind?

Preventing Suicide

A person is more likely to commit suicide if they have attempted it, or threatened to, in the past. Anyone suffering from serious physical pain, illness, physical or mental disorders, or who is caught in the spiral of alcohol or drug addiction is also at high risk. Alcohol is a powerful depressant, a fact most people are unaware of, with millions being affected by this on a daily basis.

Additionally, anyone who is grieving a serious loss, such as being fired, 'laid off', going through divorce, losing a loved one, or who has received a diagnosis of terminal or debilitating illness may be having suicidal thoughts.

If you are reading this now, and you are having thoughts of suicide, *and* especially if you are forming a plan in your mind:

- Call someone you know will help you, or
- Go to your nearest hospital emergency department or health care clinic immediately.
- Reach out to someone who can take you there, if possible.
- Tell a health care professional you are thinking of suicide.
- Call 911 if no one is available.
- You must make *reaching out* the first thing you do right now.

There is help available. Someone cares about you. Help for your problem is available. It is normal to feel ashamed of having suicidal thoughts. However, millions of people have had these thoughts and have been able to return to feeling normal and well.

Signs and Red Flags.

There are usually physical, emotional, and behavioral signs… red flags that a person is thinking about suicide. The warning signs that someone you know may be thinking about suicide can include these:
- The person says something about death, dying or suicide.
- The person suddenly starts preparing for death (giving away prized possessions, making a will, taking out life insurance.)
- Changes in sleep habits, eating patterns
- Withdrawing from regular social activities.

- Frequently expressing hopelessness or discouragement
- New patterns of reckless behavior
- A change from normal or cheerful patterns of behavior to negative and angry styles of communication
- Neglect of, or significant change in personal appearance
- Changes in personality
- Inability to enjoy time with friends, family or any other activity previously enjoyed
- Withdrawal from social activity
- Unexplained or increasing use of drugs or other mood altering substances
- Sexual promiscuity
- Previous suicide attempts

This list is not exhaustive. Ask your health care provider or go to your area's mental health association websites for common warning signs of impending suicide.

Note to professionals and students: a massive databank on mental health resources worldwide, and downloadable mental health information on everything from suicide to depression, is available on the World Health Organization's website. The link is in the Endnotes.[65]

Helping a Potentially Suicidal Person

The most important thing to do is to listen, with no judgment, and to help the person express the feelings and thoughts they are having, with a health care professional as soon as possible. Some people think that by talking about the possibility of suicide, a depressed person may actually be more likely to commit suicide. This is not the case. Talking about the feelings they are having, and getting professional help, can only assist the person on the road to recovery.

A Success Story

Susan is a middle-aged woman, well known in her community as a successful businessperson. One Sunday afternoon, I had changed my plans, and was home doing some weekly chores. The phone rang, and it was Susan asking to see me as soon as possible. I could tell by the sound of her voice that something was very wrong.

Within a short time, she was sitting in my kitchen having what used to be called a "nervous breakdown". Susan was suicidal. Until that time, I knew nothing about her long struggle with depression. She had been depressed on and off for most of her adult life and in fact, several members of her family had struggles with mental illness, including Bipolar disorder. This condition, also known as manic depression, causes the individual to feel depressed some of the time, and abnormally happy or 'euphoric', some of the time, with varying degrees of moods in between.

Susan was not only suicidal, but she had two different but very specific plans for committing suicide within the next 24 hours. It is nothing less than divine intervention that brought her to my kitchen table. I just happened to be a health care professional in her circle of friends, who knew the right questions to ask, and who happened to be home. I specifically asked her those questions early on in our conversation. The questions included:

- "Are you having thoughts of suicide?"
- "Do you have a plan to commit suicide?"

I brought her to the hospital's emergency department, where she was admitted and kept in a secure observation room until a bed was available on the psychiatric ward. Susan remained in treatment as an inpatient at the hospital for over one month.

Had Susan not picked up the phone to reach out, the outcome of the story would have been significantly different. The healthy thinking strategy in times of mental health crisis, whether you are the patient, or the family member, is always to reach out. You must reach out, and continue if necessary, until you find the person who is able to assist you to safety.

Today, well over one year later, Susan still struggles occasionally with depression and may do so for some time and perhaps over the long term. However, she knows that the better she is able to control her thoughts and redirect them to the thoughts that feel more pleasant, more of the time, the healthier she will be.

Healthier Habits

The care of our minds should receive as much focus as the care of our bodies. If not more. For even if and when one day, perhaps, in very old age, our bodies may fail us, much joy and peace remains available to us if our minds remain healthy. People facing death, still enjoying life and expressing happiness, have amazed me many times. They think differently… they have thought habits we should learn.

Developing new habits is usually a challenge. Developing more effective ways of thinking is no different, and can take several weeks or months to become part of our new and healthier self. When we are living with mental illness, this is even more of a challenge. Your health care providers will assist you in choosing the best healthy thinking methods for you, and staying on track when times are tough.

Simple, easy to remember techniques to help get your thinking back on a better-feeling wavelength, whenever you are feeling down or stressed are best. Keep in mind that positive thinking alone is not enough. Healthy thinking is a powerful, evidence-based habit, which in one way or another is at the heart of all mental fitness systems, programs, therapies and successful methods for living with or without mental health challenges. Try these:

- **Positive Visualization** (healthy daydreaming): practice creating beautiful visual images in your mind, to enjoy on a daily basis, such as a beach scene, a fragrant forest walk, a peaceful garden, or any scenario you find enjoyable. Choose scenes you would like to enjoy in real life. Practice creating and improving this visual image daily for one to two minutes as a starting point. Many people find it helpful to practice this visualization, where they are most comfortable, walking in nature, in a comfortable chair, or on a bed, perhaps with a soft towel covering their eyes. Ensuring total darkness, by covering the eyes with a soft towel or sleep mask, is very helpful in visualization, meditation or just plain relaxing.

- **Minimizing negative thoughts.** We cannot completely block out all negative thoughts. However, we can learn to push them aside and replace them with positive thoughts more often. Try this simple exercise: pre plan a pleasant thought, or one or two favorite positive images, that you will think about as a replacement thought. Lie or sit quietly with your eyes closed. As soon as a negative thought comes into your mind, think to yourself, "Hmmm… that's interesting. I'm going to think about _____ instead." Repeat this every time a negative thought pops into your mind during a short three to five minute meditation.

- **De-guilting**: whenever you have a guilty thought about a mistake you made, or how you hurt a family member or friend, move that thought 'aside' slightly. Practice saying to yourself, out loud, or with your inner voice, "That's in the past. Today is a new day, and I forgive myself." If you have not apologized to a loved one you have hurt, you may wish to do so, to help ease the burden of guilt, which you are unnecessarily carrying in your thought habits.

- **Journaling**: try keeping a journal or diary in which you express your feelings on a daily basis. Most importantly, include two or more diary entries about something that you are very grateful for each day. And on days when that may be difficult, remember that even physical capacities such as being able to see, hear and walk are things to be grateful for.

- **Staying sober**. Or at least limit you alcohol intake to 1-2 drinks per day for men, ½ - 1 drink for women (your clinician may advise you to abstain totally, for health reasons). You cannot learn or maintain healthy thinking when you are under the influence of mood-altering substances, and you cannot if you are a non-sober alcoholic. Don't believe me? Read, "When All You Have is Hope", by Frank O'Dea, Co-founder of Second Cup.[66]

- **Volunteering.** So many people all around us and in other parts of the world are in greater need than we are. Giving of ourselves is win-win: we make ourselves feel better, while at the same time helping someone else. If you have never volunteered for something, you will surprise yourself by finding new friends and possibly new skills and interests you may not realize you have. Being able to shift the focus away from our own mental health issues and negative patterns, towards the needs of others, is a powerful way to take steps back to mental health. If you are struggling with a mental health issue at this time, speak with your therapist about the possibility of volunteering. He or she will guide you in deciding when you are ready, and perhaps have some ideas about where you may want to volunteer.

- **Using Healthy Vocabulary.** Did you notice that this chapter is entitled mental wellness, and not mental illness? Try as much as possible to look for and choose the positive turn of phrase and the positive terminology for whatever it is you are speaking of.

You Are Not Your Illness

While we are on the topic of healthy vocabulary... I recently learned something about positive vocabulary from one of my clients. In our planning sessions for a symposium I was speaking at, I said something about registering clients, the "diabetics". The project manager kindly corrected me, and helped me to change a habit of negative vocabulary. Whether you have diabetes, bipolar disorder, or have suffered an amputation, *you are not your illness or your condition.* It does not define you. The respectful, empowering, more positive vocabulary would be "persons living with-------------", as in "persons living with diabetes", "people living with Alzheimer's", etc... Since that day, I am constantly working on correcting my vocabulary. This new habit is starting to feel natural, and it certainly feels like the right thing to do. Thank you, Tamara :).

Note: **To those of you, who are struggling with mental health issues at this time,** talk to your therapist about some of the above examples and how you may be able to use them in this way or in some manner he or she may suggest. Your health care provider may in fact, have other mental exercises for you to try.

Families

For families of a loved one who is facing a mental health challenge for the first time, know that there is, in most countries, a wide variety of help available for you. You, the family, must also reach out and access the support available. In the mean time, and on an ongoing basis, the same types of positive mental exercises discussed here can work for you. It is critical for family members to focus on their own health as well, when one member is mentally ill, as the stressors can be overwhelming.

Though you sometimes can be a source of great help to the individual suffering with the illness, at any given time it is important for you to accept the fact that you are doing the best you can. You are not responsible for another adult's choices, unless that person has been legally deemed mentally incapable of making their own decisions, and you are legally appointed as a guardian.

No Family – Dysfunctional Family.

If you are a person who is without or estranged from your family, you know that building relationships throughout life is crucial to your well-being. Casual and deeper friendships, a life partner and their family, joining groups and organizations, career and workplace networking… all these help you build a surrogate family, who will help you one day.

This book is not intended to deal with traumatic family dysfunction such as that of the family under the control of delusional and psychotic persons.

If you are a victim of incest, mind control,
beatings or other abuse,
seek help as soon as possible.

You are isolated: you are not guilty of anything. You are innocent.

Millions of people have come out of dysfunctional family situations,
and you can too.

You deserve a better life: you can be free and safe.

Children's Help Phone Numbers

If you are abused in any way, call for help now.
Call a child abuse or family violence agency for help.
Here are some numbers you can call anytime of the day or
night in Canada, and the USA:

- **Emergency: 911**
- **Child Help USA at 1-800-422-4453.**
- **Kids Help Phone Line Canada: 1-800-668-6868**

You do not live in Canada or the United States?
Write down the children's help organizations in your
country here:

Physical Triggers

The study of anatomy, physiology, or biochemistry would bring you knowledge about the beneficial effects physical activity has on our mental state. Hundreds (probably thousands now) of studies have shown that people who suffer from depression benefit immensely from physical exercise. Though it is not always easy, the developing of a daily habit of 30 minutes of exercise makes a significant difference in our well-being. However, if you begin the practice of 30 minutes of mild to moderate exercise, such as walking, on a daily basis, pay attention to the changes you will experience. Notice how different you feel emotionally, during the walk, and immediately afterwards. Notice how different you feel for hours, and as the weeks go by.

Do you sometimes find that it is difficult to motivate yourself to take that 30-minute walk? I have a suggestion for you, and first, keep in mind; it takes approximately 30 days to develop a new habit. And because we are human, it is always easy for us to "fall off the wagon" and undo that habit as well. Mental health takes work, but it is satisfying work. The suggestion is as follows. Even if you think you "just don't have the energy" to go for that 30-minute walk, today, at least do this. *Put on* your exercise or walking clothes… the sneakers or running shoes, the pants and shirt you would normally wear and even the hat, if that is the case. The simple practice of "getting on the gear" will probably have the trigger effect of getting you out the door for some exercise, or at least 10 minutes of walking room-to-room and up/down the stairs in your house.

Brain Plasticity

"Your mind works on getting you what it sees."
Dr. Daniel Amen. Author of "Magnificent Mind at Any Age"

Science has made major breakthroughs in the understanding of how the mind actually functions. More importantly, we now know that we were wrong in originally believing that whatever brain potential we were born with was static.

I included Dr. Amen's quote above, as he has joined the ranks of the highly respected scientists, physicians, nurses and allied health professionals who are spreading a common message. Hypnosis, meditation, Emotional Freedom Technique, (EFT[67]), Cognitive Behavioral Therapy (CBT), visualization... all of these change the brain in a positive way. This can be seen using imaging technology such as MRI (Magnetic Resonance Imaging). Some of Dr. Amen's 'prescriptions' include the basics of healthy thinking, such as telling patients to think about five things they are grateful for every day and to meditate on these every day, for a period of three weeks. His research shows that after this period of time, people will experience a significant increase in happiness.[68]

We now know the brain has the capacity to change itself, to create new pathways and build new neurons. With MRI, we can see into the brain to observe the functioning of individual cell groups. We see that the brain can reshape itself and establish healthier and even new functions, or reestablish old ones. One 5-year old girl had one hemisphere (one-half) of her brain removed due to a grave seizure disorder she had from the time she was a toddler. She thrilled her medical team and the scientific community after half her brain was cut out: bright and happy, she *walked* out of the hospital days later, functioning well, and enjoyed continuing improvement in functioning for years to come. She is now a normal 10-year-old child, thanks to the miracle of her own brain's plasticity. [69]

The excitement around the concept of brain plasticity is growing, thanks to the work of Dr. Norman Doidge, psychiatrist, psychoanalyst, and researcher. In his groundbreaking book, "The Brain That Changes Itself: Stories of Personal Triumph from the Frontiers of Brain Science"[70], Dr. Doidge presents irrefutable evidence, fantastic and inspiring case studies and clinical research of many cases where people have had *spectacular results by changing the way they think.*

Dr. Doidge explains in plain language, the miraculous power of our brain and its thinking function. He presents cases where those living with blindness have learned to see, people living with deafness learned to hear, and where people who have suffered strokes many years previously, experienced amazing improvements in their function and abilities. He also bravely speaks out speaks out on how the brain maps of millions of people are being negatively reshaped by exposure to pornography, and the long-term effects of this preoccupation or addiction, on individuals and our society as a whole. Our brains are being de-sensitized, to feed the moneymaking machine of the pornography industry. He works with men trying desperately to free themselves from the now online-fed addiction.

In particular, it is very encouraging to explore what Dr. Doidge and his colleagues have to say about specific thinking strategies and how they can help in cases of depression. For those of you who live with depression, I encourage you to speak with your clinician, if you are not already doing so, and ask about specific thinking exercises that may be helpful for you.

Dr. Emile Coué

One of the most recognized (and often satirized), and still widely used mental exercises is a simple statement created by Dr. Emile Coué, often considered the first of the modern positive Psychologists. He believed and taught we have strength we can access to overcome negative feelings and emotions, such as sadness and overwhelm. He developed a short sentence, a self-talk mantra if you will, and it is reported that he would only take you on as a new patient, if you agreed to repeat this phrase over and over to yourself daily. Here is the much-maligned phrase:

"Every day in every way I'm getting better and better."[71]

Dr. Coué suggested that this phrase be repeated for several minutes at a time, as long as it took, he taught, to decrease the depressed or negative feeling originally present. Notice that he does not suggest the patient repeat phrases, which are in no way possible or true in the present tense. He did *not* for example, tell the patient to say,

"Today, I am happy. I will always be happy. And I will never be depressed again."

Though his writings may be outdated, and case study presentations anecdotal, Dr. Coué's beliefs and logic speak from a place of truth. The wave within the scientific community now supporting this basic concept is heartening to say the least. My dying patients were right. Mahatma Ghandi was right. My mother was right. There is *something* to the repetitive use of uplifting thought, which can no longer be denied.

Is There a Positive Aspect to Depression?

What?! Healthy thinkers look for genuine, positive aspects in even the most negative situation. Though this is not always possible, or even a respectful suggestion for someone in deep despair, I leave you with the words of Thomas Moore. He is one of the few leading philosophers courageously exploring depression, in a quest for meaning. He proposes it has something to teach all of us, whether we are experiencing at, or we are part of the circle of someone living with depression. In no way suggesting that professional care is not required, Moore sees the seeking of meaning within depression an idea worthy of exploration by mental health professionals. The following words are from his "Care of the Soul" chapter, "Gifts of Depression."[72]

"Depression grants the gift of experience not as a literal fact, but as an attitude toward yourself. You get a sense of having lived through something, of being older and wiser." Thomas Moore

...and the philosopher is not alone:

"While many people see depression as a dirty word, people are their most creative with depression since it seems that there is nothing to lose."
Dr. Mehmet Oz[73]

"The dullness that comes with depression and the depression itself, is part of being human - those dark times need to be felt in order to appreciate the good times."
Montel Williams, on Multiple Sclerosis and Depression[74]

I leave this chapter with a meditative poem for you.

A Ray of Light

A Meditative Poem for Mental Wellness

Think. A ray of light,
bursting through a clouded sky,
bringing comfort,
hope, to still a cry.

See. A lighthouse clear,
across the lonely bay,
conquers fear
in those who lost their way.

Hear, the voice of ones who care,
calling you from where you roam,
on lonely streets, that lead nowhere,
calling you safe, calling you home.

Know. We will not rest until the day
you laugh with us in the sun,
until the day when peace,
for all minds and souls, together we have won.

by Gisèle Guénard ©2009

Notes:

Chapter 2

Death and Dying

"Now he has departed from this strange world a little ahead of me. That means nothing. People like us, who believe in physics, know that the distinction between past, present and future is only a stubbornly persistent illusion."

Albert Einstein's letter to the family of his lifelong friend Michele Besso, after learning of his death, [75]

100% Guaranteed

We are all going to die. There it is. Not only are we guaranteed to die, but also, for the majority of us, we will face the death of a loved one at some point in our life. I served at the bedside as a registered nurse in the 70s and 80s, before many of the wonder drugs and cancer therapies we are now using were developed. I remember many patients. The 70-year-old woman dying of lung cancer, in a private room at the end of the hall, virtually comatose: the only movement she made in her last days and hours was moving her hand up towards her mouth, held as if a cigarette was between her two fingers. I remember a young mother dying of breast cancer, and her husband not making it back in time to be with her in the last moments. I remember being the first to administer intravenous morphine on a 'regular medical floor', and not in intensive care, at our hospital. It was for a man who was dying a painful death from metastatic cancer.

When we work directly with people in need, teamwork and dedication is 'mental caring' work. There were 65 patients on our unit, with every diagnosis from myocardial infarction (heart attack), to dementia, pneumonia, every kind of cancer you can think of, and a few post-operative people here and there. At that time, there was no special unit for the care of patients living with cancer. We administered chemotherapy at the patient's bedside, whether they were in a private room or a ward with three other patients. We mixed the toxic drugs on the patient's bedside table, with no masks and no ventilation hoods. Our unit was typical of units everywhere, a crazy busy place, where our assignment included up to 12 patients, and every shift was life and death. We worked at staying upbeat, and we were successful at it.

I share this information to give you reassurance, confidence and hope: should you ever be faced with the need for cancer care, or care for any terminal illness, remember the following. Though wherever humans work, there are incidents of poor communication, medication errors and system failure, the overwhelming majority of people working in the health care system today, are highly skilled, caring individuals, *who do not rest until your needs are met.* Great advances have been made in all aspects of palliative care in the past 20 years. I encourage you to get informed about these aspects as they pertain to your particular situation or illness. Knowledge is power. Power for positive change… even in end-of-life care. But first, a reality check.

Life Expectancy

Fill out this form or have a family meeting. with everyone doing the same:

I would like to live to be _____ years of age, with the following abilities and enjoyable aspects to my life, as I grow into old age:

1.

2.

3.

4.

5.

Etc…

In order to live the above experience, I am making the following daily choices:

1.

2.

3.

4.

5.

Etc….

Makes one think, does it not?

What Determines Your Health… and When You Will Die?

It is largely where you

1. are born,

2. grow,

3. live,

4. work,

plus

5. your age, and…

6. the health system you have access to.

The distribution of money, power and resources, locally, nationally and globally, shapes the above six Determinants of Health, which are shaping your destiny. All the other elements, which contribute to your life expectancy, tumble down from those six determinants. If this comes as a surprise to you, review the simplified life expectancy table on the next page. This information is a current snapshot of life expectancy at birth, in randomly selected countries. The World Health Organization's (WHO) tables are much more detailed, and a source of information for all health organizations and planning agencies worldwide. [76]

Though at this time, we have serious concerns about the decline in life expectancy for some population groups due to alarming obesity rates, especially in children, it is important to keep things in perspective. At the turn of the 20th century, Canadians for example, are lucky if they made it to their 50th birthday. By 1922, the average Canadian man was living until 59 and the average woman until 61.[77] What are we doing as individuals, starting with what we are thinking about on a day-to-day basis, in order to increase our chances in the life expectancy game?

We generally do not think about our life expectancy until we are sick, or getting on in years. Is this healthy? As a glimpse of the current global state of affairs, here are just a few statistics from the WHO 2008 data[78]. Food for thought…

- Differences in life expectancy between the richest and poorest countries now exceed 40 years.
- The number of people with access to safe drinking water rose from 4.1 billion in 1190 to 5.7 billion in 2006.
- In Nairobi, the under 5 mortality rate is below 15 per 1000 in the high-income area. In a slum *in the same city*, the rate is 254 per 1000.
- In Europe, 39 out of 100,000 children died before their fifth birthday in 1990. The figure is now 27 out of 100,000.
- Maternal mortality has barely changed since 1990.
- 27 countries reported a reduction of up to 50% in the number of malaria cases between 1990 and 2006.

The big picture has some bad news, some good news, and thankfully thousands of people applying their thought, energy and attention to positive change in all of the above areas.

Life expectancy Snapshot 2009

Country	Life Expectancy (in Years). Selected Countries		
	Women	Men	Both Sexes
Afghanistan	42	41	42
Australia	84	79	82
Brazil	76	70	73
Cambodia	61	58	61
Canada	83	78	81
China	75	72	74
Côte d'Ivoire	57	52	54
Egypt	70	66	68
Finland	83	76	79
France	84	77	81
Haiti	64	59	62
India	65	63	64
Indonesia	70	67	68
Jamaica	74	69	72
Japan	86	79	83
Lesotho	47	43	45
Mali	50	47	49
Peru	77	75	76
Sierra Leone	43	39	41
South Africa	55	52	54
Switzerland	84	79	82
UK	82	77	80
USA	81	76	78
Zimbabwe	44	45	45

Source: VisionarEase.com . From World Health Organization's World Health Statistics. 2009

Change Sometimes Hurts before it Feels Good

Sometimes it takes a wake-up call... an illness, or perhaps an injury, to make us change habits and practices we have that could be damaging our health. It is a conscious thought-action process to do so. It is difficult to change long-standing habits, but *oh, so worth it.*

> It is more important to know what kind of patient has the disease than what kind of disease the patient has. Sir William Osler

What kind of patient would you be?

Rose's story

This is the true story about a courageous friend of mine who bravely applied her declining energy to thinking as effectively as possible throughout her end of life journey.

Just over a year ago, I learned from a mutual friend that Rose (not her real name) had been diagnosed with terminal cancer. She had just turned 50. I was living in another community, we moved in different circles, and we had not seen each other in years. She had been complaining of left-sided lower pelvic pain for some time. It was advanced ovarian cancer. Her case was far beyond the possibility of a cure, with large painful tumors growing in her body, the cancer having metastasized to other areas.

In the final months of her life, once she had accepted that the end was inevitable, she made a decision. You see, she had three children, young adults, between the ages of 18 and 21. She knew that the best way to face this difficult role, for her was to be brave. She made a decision to be as positive as possible for her family, and she hoped to teach them some valuable life lessons along the way.

A mutual friend, an expert in the field of death, dying and grief, agreed to be part of her care circle and to help her through. He sat with her for hours, helping her talk about all of the things that were still in her heart; her fears, her questions, her beliefs, her worries for her children. He helped her prepare for death, and he helped her build on her natural spirit of gratefulness and joy.

She experienced major breakthroughs of understanding, was accepting the inevitable and had found peace. Though she still had pain and terrible symptoms, she faced each day with thankfulness. One day, her oncologist told her that he had never met anyone like her... no patient with her spirit, and that *she was inspiring them.*

We shared many wonderful moments together, and I am fortunate to have been in her circle. She loved music... classic rock, blues, folk... all the stuff we grew up with. I brought my autoharp in for her one day, and played "Wondering Where the Lions Are", by Bruce Cockburn[79]. We both cried... I could hardly sing it. She asked me to play it at her funeral. I said I would, though I really did not know if I would be able to.

When the day came, I was preparing to go to the church to say goodbye to her. After having decided that I would not be able to play, I changed my mind. The decision to play at the funeral was so clear and so vivid in my mind; it was as if she spoke to me and said, with a twinkle in her eye as usual... "You *promised*, Gisèle..." I took out my autoharp and practiced a couple of times. I know her spirit was with me, because though it was difficult, I was able to perform her song well, and help others share the experience that I had with her.

There is a great lesson here. As my friend Charmaine, a social worker, Reiki practitioner and business leader, shared, [80]

"We are sure of only two things in life, that we are born, and that we die. What we do with what's in between is up to us."

Though I knew it at a superficial level, after living the experience with

Rose, the knowledge that it is possible to enjoy life even in our dying days, is for me, confirmed. Even at the very end of our days.

Note: Ovarian cancer is the most serious of all gynecological cancers, often going undetected until it is too late. In Canada, Over 2500 women are diagnosed every year; and 700 women succumb to this disease. Symptoms are varied, vague and easily missed.

There is no screening test to detect it. But when found early – and treated – the ovarian cancer survival rate is 90%.[81]

From Grieving "in Stages" to Moving On

Dr. Elizabeth Kubler-Ross, well over 30 years ago, presented her (now disputed) model of "five stages" of grief we supposedly experience, in a certain order, when faced with death and dying.[82] Grief recovery specialists now provide care using other models as the base for their practice, models more helpful to the person facing death. Kubler-Ross' terminology is still widely used, however, and there is value in understanding her initial intent. The terms she presented and their general meaning are still widely included in day-to-day work by health care professionals. One registered nurse I interviewed stated that the Kubler-Ross model was taught verbatim, in her undergraduate course, only a few years ago.

There are great variations in our experiences of the death of cousin, a friend, a sibling or a parent, with the loss of a child being the most traumatic. In addition, no death or grief experience is ever as cut and dried as "five defined stages". Yet, you will hear these terms at some point when faced with death and dying. This is my interpretation and commentary around Kubler-Ross' initial theory. And though many now deny that any of this plays out in the real world, you can decide if it looks familiar or not.

Denial

Just as the word implies, faced with the knowledge that we are experiencing a terminal illness, or when told of the death of a loved one, the first thing that springs to mind in my experience, and that of others I have seen in this situation, is to think, blurt out, or make a statement such as,

- "No! It can't be true"
- "You're lying!"
- "It's a mistake! It must be someone else!"

I experienced this at the time of my older brother's premature death. My younger brother had called to tell me that Michel had just been killed on his motorcycle. Not only did I react by crying out into the telephone "No! No! It can't be true!", when I got to the hospital, I went to the emergency room, and *asked to see my brother Mike.* I told the nurse that I was quite sure there was a mistake... and that he was in fact *in intensive care.* The truth was that he was lying in the morgue.

It is not uncommon to see people drop to the floor, unable to bear the trauma of being told a loved one has died. Shock, confusion, and even physical symptoms such as nausea, vomiting and chest pain are often seen. It is my opinion that what we call denial is often more like a profound expression of disbelief. I see it as a defence mechanism: at that moment, *we have an intense desire for this horrific fact to be a bad dream, simply not real.* And we want the information presented to us to be wrong, a cruel mistake. Our denial response takes us from there onward, and may be serving a purpose we do not yet fully understand.

Anger

We cannot remain in denial forever. Faced with death and dying, anger is common. We are angry at others, angry at ourselves, angry at professionals caring for us, angry at the world. We look to blame someone.

An elderly man I was caring for, who had very little family, was crying one day when I went into his room. He was struggling through the last months of his life, with metastatic cancer. Initially, I assumed that he was crying, because of either pain, or sadness about his diagnosis. After a few minutes, he began to open up, and to tell me about the abuse he suffered as a child, the beatings, and the neglect. The overriding message in his plea was "Why?", "Why me? I was just a little boy…" He did find peace before he died, once again thanks to an expert, caring circle of end-of-life caregivers.

Bargaining

In the case of imminent death, it is common for us to offer an exchange of some sort, or bargain, in an attempt to buy us more time. I was in the room when a patient, facing death within a few weeks, pleaded with the oncologist (cancer specialist),

"Isn't there some kind of experimental treatment I can take? If I can only have a few months… if I can only have the summer…"

Depression

This stage is that of true grief. The dying person now understands that death is approaching, and becomes quieter, sometimes crying, sometimes simply wanting to be left alone. In fact, it may be better termed "deep sadness", and often comes and goes throughout the dying or grief period. It is common for health care givers to express sadness at this time as well. Emotions are highly contagious, and I believe there is therapeutic value in the caregiver appropriately expressing some level of feeling, which is similar to that of the patient, when it is genuine.

Acceptance

Finally, for most, comes acceptance. For those of us who are fortunate enough to have the gift of time with our dying loved ones, we probably experience this period of peace and understanding. I have seen patients enjoying interactions with loved ones and caregivers during this phase, chatting, even joking, and clearly enjoying their last days.

The Kubler-Ross model does not take into account cultural issues and individual characteristics of each patient's situation, such as relationships or type of illness. This is one reason the validity of her ideas has been widely disputed. There still is a strong element of her initial writings in the work of more current researchers.

J.W. Worden

J. W. Worden's work is more current and presents a very practical way of thinking through the tasks of grieving. [83] He presents a model of grieving as a series of tasks we need to 'work hard at,' to complete. They are,

Accepting the Reality of the Loss

Regardless of the mechanism we used to get there, we must find a way of accepting that the truth is the truth. We must accept, for example that we *are* dying, if that is the case, or perhaps that our loved one has died.

Experiencing the Pain of Grief

To move forward through grief, we need to experience the pain of it. Initially, this can be numbed by our denial, disbelief, and the physical process of shock. We often see this at the scene of an accident where the person does not realize they have lost a limb, for example.

Adjusting to Life Without your Loved One

Our lives change after the loss of a loved one. It may be hard for you to believe this, if you are now in the early days of grief, but the pain subsides eventually. We begin to find ways to accommodate the changes in our lives.

This takes time and requires a degree of detachment from the loved one. It is often a time of great struggle. We may feel guilty for beginning to move on, for not always thinking about our loved one every second of the day.

Moving on

This "task" mercifully contains within it the experience of joy in our lives, once again. We make decisions. We feel a rediscovered sense of contentment. However, guilt or regret does surface, often when we 'feel bad for not thinking of the loved one' as much as we previously were.

The important thing to remember, with all of these stages, phases and tasks, is that there is an end to it all. We do grow; we do become stronger for having lived through it. If our own death is facing us, we are not alone. We will all walk down that path one day. The importance of family, friends and support groups cannot be overstated with issues around end-of-life. Throughout life, it is of paramount importance to continue to build relationships and help others: in turn, we are helped when we too, face the music.

Miscarriage

Death, at any age, is still death. For the parents expecting a child, and especially for the mother, miscarriage brings with it all of the elements and experiences one would expect when faced with the death of any loved one. Though the grieving period may not last as long, support is still needed. The most un-healthy thing we can do as family and friends, though we mean well, is to minimize the experience simply because "it was just a foetus", or "it was for the best, there was probably something wrong with it". Current research supports the fact that miscarriage can be linked to significant and possibly long-term psychological consequences.[84]

A mother experiencing miscarriage is not sad. She is devastated. All of the typical symptoms of grief, and even depression, can be felt to some degree after miscarriage, including sadness, hopelessness, and losing interest in activities. Difficulty concentrating, loss of appetite, insomnia, weight loss or gain, a feeling of emptiness, nausea, pain, including that associated with the miscarriage itself, and other physical symptoms are common. Follow up with the physician, nurse practitioner, midwife or obstetrician is always required.

It is also common for relationships to be strained around the time of miscarriage. Support groups for couples exist in larger centers, and even getting together to talk with other couples who have experienced miscarriage, is a very positive approach to this difficult period.

A Note To New Mothers: If you are still feeling signs of extreme sadness, depression, overwhelm, or the inability to cope, several weeks after your miscarriage, visit your primary health care provider again.

An Oak Tree Grows

It is normal and appropriate to grieve deeply after miscarriage. The fact that the miscarriage may have been very early on is irrelevant. After all, you were already bonded, and feeling the love for the child growing within you. There is nothing embarrassing about needing professional help after miscarriage. This is a major life event. Going through it with whatever help you need, will help you to move forward, and even help you through your next pregnancy.

My daughter and her husband were expecting their first baby. Around the tenth week and after several days of excruciating pain, she lost the baby. We are a tight-knit family and helped them grieve as best we could… all of us… parents, siblings and friends. We were all there as much as they needed us, and helped them through it together.

An oak tree now grows in the backyard of their home, in honour of the child. That little tree is growing like a weed, and now, a little boy, born just over a year later will soon be playing in the sandbox under that tree.

Within families, healthy thinking in times of trouble is synonymous with acting on the love we have for one another.

Normal or Not?

It is easy to think we are over reacting when tragedy strikes. Here are a few facts to think about:

1. **Remember, that denial and shock are normal, and temporary.** These are probably coping and defence mechanisms. Allowing denial to be expressed, as disturbing as it sometimes is to observe, is best. There is no reason to feel ashamed at the denial outbursts. When you wish to help somebody experiencing painful denial, being there, offering emotional support or comfort, and helping with day-to-day activities in the initial hours or days, goes a long way in helping the person get through the pain.

2. **Know ahead of time, that feelings of anger will probably emerge.** Expressing these feelings with someone in your care circle will help you tremendously. If someone is expressing anger in your presence, or perhaps even towards you while grieving, keep in mind: it is not about you, *it is about the trauma they are living.* It is helpful to respond with comments such as,

"I can't know exactly what you're feeling, but I do know it is very difficult. Is there something I can do?"

3. **During deep sadness, it is best to allow the person time for grieving.** They must process the experience for themselves. Though well meaning, attempts to "cheer a person up" with superficial comments or jokes, are not recommended. It is best to communicate in a supportive manner. Instead, use comments such as,

"I'm here for you. How can I help you today?"

4. **Move on at your own pace.** As you move through loss and grieving, you will eventually begin to have feelings and thoughts such as,

"Others need and want my attention, my love and my help. Giving my attention to other people does not mean that I love my lost loved one any less."

This is normal and healthy. Build on those thoughts, emotions and feelings.

The Value of Sadness

Catherine Cannon, a licensed Grief Recovery Specialist offers this wisdom.

"The Grief Recovery Institute discourages the concept of the stages of grief; we believe that everyone grieves in their own way based on the uniqueness of the relationship, and that many people do not experience all of the stages. In addition, the idea of "stages" implies that there is a timeline to grieving and we know that time without process does not facilitate recovery from loss.

Carl Jung said, "I am not what's happening to me. I am what I choose to be." If we take responsibility for our reactions to events, we can choose to accept and let go. However, if we adhere to a state of feeling victimized by circumstances or by others, recovery is not possible. Recovery does not mean that one will never feel sadness due to loss, but that the sadness will no longer be considered a bad thing. Our socialization has led us to believe that sadness is a bad; if we can come to a state of honouring sadness, a sweetness will enter it and feelings of love and connection will be part of the sadness. I've come to realize that my goal in life is not happiness; it is serenity. Sadness can be (and should be) an integral part of that sense of peace. [85]

At the Edge of the Abyss

I have rarely encountered anyone who did not have, or develop, a belief in a higher power at the end of his or her days. Accessing one's own belief system... that there *is* something... a Higher Power... can empower *us*.

There are as many terms for the Higher Power as there are societies and cultures in the world. I have come to realize that somehow, we are a part of that Spirit. Through the grief process, we often feel that spirit, that connection within, and feel prompted to *ask for* help. When asking for help from God, the Spirit, the Source, I have always received help. The answer has not always been what I thought I wanted. However each time, and yet in retrospect, good *did* come from it. Peace always returned. New paths always revealed themselves... paths that I would not or could not have taken, had the prayer been answered exactly as I wished it.

Sanctuary

There is a practice in many philosophies and religions, of providing sanctuary. In the free world, we are at liberty to reach out for help from spiritual leaders from whatever source we feel drawn to. Yes, though it is true that deep shame and unfathomable human error does exist within the ranks of religious leaders, as it does in the ranks of other areas of society, take heart. There is still much that is good in religious organizations.

Faced with the imminent death of a loved one, or your own, I encourage you to seek the counsel of respected spiritual leaders, perhaps one trained in multi-faith support, or of your own faith. You may be more comfortable with someone who can offer a purely humanistic approach. No one, and certainly no religious leader is perfect. Imperfect as we are, we can still help each other in times of need. Grief and grief work has been known to bring out the best in the most imperfect of us. A man of the cloth, who used to visited the sick and dying in a hospital I worked in was often the target of gossip. His life was not perfect, and his failings were well known. However, the joy and peace he brought to those people whom he ministered to in their dying days, was a clear and present reality.

Inner sanctuary

There is a sanctuary we have access to, which does not require a building, the assistance of another, nor does it require organized religion of any type. It is our own inner sanctuary, accessible through simple meditation. Once you have learned to *be still and to go within*, and to experience the peace present within your inner self, you will be much better prepared to face difficult times.

When we visit friends or loved ones gravely ill, in hospitals or nursing homes, we sometimes seek out a chapel. Most health care facilities have such a room, often nondenominational, to which anyone can go and find a sanctuary in which to think quietly, pray or meditate. There is a reason for this. Health care planners have realized that there is more to meditation than rote repetition of words, and that there is a need for sanctuary space in our facilities. There is health and great strength to be accessed through these practices, an example of which is at the end of this chapter.

Prescription for Excellence

One of our concerns is that the health care system will fail us when we are gravely ill or dying. We fear errors, we fear being neglected, and we fear pain. Know that there have been impressive advances in our ability to care for the dying. Any facility, which is delivering high quality end-of-life care, is doing so thanks to dedicated and competent health care professionals and support staff, as well as the leaders of those organizations. The leaders of organizations, which are acknowledged as excellent *by their clientele*, think differently. They apply their energy, attention and focus to providing the best, in this case end-of-life, services available with their current resources.

Palliative care is a complex specialty area, which, when it is 'done right', is provided by people with an extensive and precise knowledge base and expert communication skills. These professionals are able to assess every need the dying person is experiencing, and implement the best care available at the time.

For leaders in the health care system interested in ideas for organizational change and development, ideas that would help make their organization the absolute best place to be when one requires end-of-life care, I would recommend Dr. Michael Rachlis' works, and in particular, his national bestseller "Prescription for Excellence: How Innovation is Saving Canada's Health Care System"[86]. He offers a clear picture of what is *not* working at this time with end-of-life care, and solutions that all societies could be exploring for implementation. "Dying patients know what they want," he says, with much of it falling into the following five categories:

- Adequate control of pain and symptoms
- Avoiding inappropriate prolongation of dying
- Achieving a sense of control
- Relieving the burden from loved ones
- Strengthening personal relationships

His message is that a health care system which is effectively planned and organized, will help dying patients, as well as their loved ones, achieve these goals... healthy thinking in leadership, indeed.

The Power of Common Experience

What kinds of stories are you hearing? We now have access to an almost infinite number of books, films and recordings about people who have walked treacherous roads before us. People, who have gone through struggles similar to ours, have recorded their stories for history. There is nothing like truly "getting into" an inspiring story that has elements of our own to help us through one more day.

If you are too ill or unable to go seek out these resources on your own, there may be someone who could help you with this. Most hospitals, long-term care facilities and hospices have televisions, DVD players, computers, and whatever technology is required to help you spend some time enjoying inspiring films, documentaries, or to listen to stories which will give you strength.

The effectiveness of this strategy seems to come from the simple fact that taking our thoughts away from our own crisis, and spending enjoyable time thinking about the story as it unfolds before us, can help us find courage in others' experiences.

Support groups for persons experiencing terminal illness and their families are also a great resource for help in accessing these materials.

Calling on Angels

For those diagnosed with terminal illness who I have had the honour of being close to, when graced with the luxury of time between the diagnosis and death, they did come to acceptance and peace. Granted, it may be difficult for you to imagine it can be so at this time. For those whom I witnessed expressing joy and having fun with their visitors, know this. They were thinking differently. Guided imagery is effective and used worldwide in the support of death and dying. We need to 'get through it' as best we can, with whatever works for us. If it is meditation, great. If it is calling on angels, great. If friends and social activities are what you need, go for it. If it is re-connecting with your spiritual beliefs, I know you will find solace there as well. Whatever strategy you use needs to offer you some measure of *feeling better*, an inner peace.

The bottom line is that we do not "do this dying part" very well. We all know that we will die someday. We know that if we are aware of it ahead of time, we will experience sadness. We also know that we will experience sadness through the loss of our loved ones. Why we do not better prepare for death knowing all of this, has its root in good old denial, and avoidance of pain. We can prepare better... starting with our thinking habits.

Notes:

Sanctuary Meditation

This meditation exercise can be used in situations involving impending death or terminal diagnosis. You may want to speak to your primary caregiver, complementary therapy professional or a grief counsellor, to help you with this technique, and perhaps learn other supportive mental exercises.

It is helpful to wear earplugs and eye coverings for this exercise.

1. If possible, find a quiet place where you can be alone. If this is not possible, get as physically comfortable as you can.

2. Close your eyes, and practice ignoring any sound reaching you.

3. Begin breathing a little more deeply than you were. Be still and comfortable, with your eyes closed. Enjoy this relaxation for one to three minutes.

4. Practice *letting go* of all thoughts as they come, by returning your attention to simple breathing. When a thought comes into your mind, imagine a peaceful, calming color instead. Practice imagining that the mental screen of your imagination is that colour. Your mental screen is so big that you cannot see the edges. Some people prefer that their inner mental screen is a variety of colors.

5. Next, create a visual in your mind, of yourself looking and feeling at peace, effortlessly going about daily activities. Focus on this visual scene until you can clearly see yourself feeling better, looking better, and feeling peaceful.

6. If you are facing a terminal diagnosis, create either a mental scene you enjoy, or one of yourself experiencing this life and death event in the best possible way you can imagine, under the circumstances. The second option will be challenging for you if you have not accepted the diagnosis. At that time, you may find it a great comfort.

Chapter 3

Catastrophe

"The last of the great human freedoms is

the power to choose how you react to what ever happens."

Victor Franko, Jewish concentration camp philosopher

When All is Lost

...or so it seems.

Many years ago, I experienced a catastrophe, which at the time was devastating to me. As we often find however, this event brought me to new paths, which I had no choice but to follow, and which in time brought me joy.

It was in the early 80s, when my children were very little. I received a phone call from my sister-in-law, telling me that our home had burned down to the ground. Miraculously, no one was seriously injured. Every possession I treasured, however, from irreplaceable photos of my girls as babies and toddlers, to family documents, to the antique boudoir dresser given to me by my mother was gone. Everything. All reduced to rubble and ash. We were not wealthy, though we did have basic insurance. It took years to recover financially from this loss, as in the same period, my husband and I went our separate ways.

How does a person get through this type of catastrophe? When multiple stressors make it seem as if you are living in a pressure cooker. Eventually, the worst of it did pass. The overwhelming levels of stress did diminish, and life went on. I was able to make excellent decisions for my daughters and for myself. I learned many lessons about life, and I learned much about myself, my wonderful family and friends and the strength within us through that difficult time.

Avoiding Isolation

"Why didn't you call me?!" How often have you heard these words, or perhaps said them yourself? We avoid asking people to help us in times of trouble, and others avoid asking us to help them. There is great temptation, when faced with catastrophe or any traumatic experience, to isolate ourselves. Perhaps we feel that we are supposed to be able to "handle things on our own" and find our way through the darkest of times without 'bothering' other people. Maybe we do not want to bother other people because they may have problems of their own. Perhaps we are confused and simply not thinking logically, not thinking in a healthy way at that time. Regardless of the root cause... *beware*. It is very common to want to isolate ourselves in times of trouble.

Self-imposed isolation can take many forms. It can be complete in that a person totally shuts themselves off from others. Many years ago, after the death of her beloved husband, my favourite aunt did exactly that. We were neighbours, and it was winter. My brothers and I played out doors every evening after dinner. On this particular night, bundled up, we walked towards her house to 'check out the rink'. Her house was on the lake, beside the skating rink my dad and brothers made every year in front of it. We all thought she had gone away to be with her sister in her grief. When we approached her home, we were terrified by a blue light flickering from inside. Our imaginations in overdrive, we ran home, breathless by the time we reached Mom & Dad. As it turns out, when my father went to see what was going on, my aunt was there after all, alone in the dark, grieving. She had decided to stay there and she did not want other people to know. Deciding to isolate herself in her grief, she simply wanted to be alone.

Avoiding any discussion of the issue is another way to isolate ourselves during and after catastrophe. By doing so, we can avoid having to make decisions about the future. We can circumvent having to make changes. This can spiral, however, into a style of thinking that holds a person back from being able to enjoy all that life has to offer.

After the fire, I was very fortunate. I had caring extended family who took us in. Though I tried to refuse initially, thinking the rebuilding would start soon, my uncle insisted that my daughters and I stay with him and his family as long as we needed to. Now keep in mind, they already had a large family and a busy farm to run. I gratefully accepted his offer of help and stayed there for a month. The relief of not having to do everything on my own and of having family around to help with child care and to keep my mind off the negative, was a comforting and healing force.

People often refuse help offered. We can even delay reaching out and seeking help until it is too late, until greater harm has come to us, or our families. The ability to accept and when necessary to seek out, and accept the help of others is critical in times of crisis. For the one extending the offer of help, it is sometimes necessary to 'make' the person accept the assistance, for his or her own safety, such as when an involuntary psychiatric admission is required.

Accepting the Now - Building Block for Resilience

Al is 96. He has managed to remain independent for most of his life, only recently requiring the assistance of family members to help with heavy tasks. He has made it this far, he will tell you, despite two world wars, losing many loved ones, widowhood, illnesses and major surgery, weakening eyesight, hearing, and many aches and pains. I asked him how he got through the hard times in life. He answered with the simplest wisdom of all, "You just have to take it as it comes," he said, "you just have to take it as it comes and go on."

Is this a learned, Zen like attitude, something that only comes with age? Or is it something that even the young can learn?

You can relax. There is no need to start burning incense and shedding all your possessions. The main building blocks of acceptance are *awareness* and *letting go*. Try a Letting Go strategy the next time something upsetting enters into your life experience. Practice at first with mild or minor irritations:

1. As soon as you feel a negative reaction to an incident or to what someone has said, (or even a bad memory), stop for a few seconds and simply think clearly, "Hmmm… that is triggering a (guilty, frightened, sad, angry, etc.) feeling for me." Allow yourself to feel the negative reaction, the feeling itself, for a moment.

2. Next, think or acknowledge that you know for sure this feeling will not remain with you forever.

3. Now practice letting go of the feeling, or dropping it and moving on to something else. You know that it is possible to let go of negative

feelings. You have done it many times before. It feels much the same as when you say, in response to something you really cannot control, "Oh well…" and move on to something else in your day.

4. As soon as you feel the weight of the bad feeling lighten, take note and congratulate yourself for having successfully *let go*.

The more you practice acceptance or 'letting go' strategies, the more they become second nature for you, strengthening your resilience in the most difficult of times.

Decision Making in Times of Crisis

Emergency training, whether developed for workers on the factory floor, or leaders of large organizations and governments, always involves good thinking, and in particular, decision-making skills. The better we can prepare ourselves to make decisions when under pressure, the more successfully we will deal with catastrophe. Our decisions may not always be the absolute best, but we must make decisions in times of crisis. Those who do not, risk perishing. Let's look at a few examples.

The October Crisis.

It was October of 1970. I was in the 10th grade, and our nation was riveted to the news. Terrorists had kidnapped British diplomat James Cross in Québec and cabinet minister Pierre Laporte. Pierre Elliott Trudeau, prime minister of Canada (1968-79 and 1980-84 – our longest standing prime minister), made a choice. He invoked the War Measures Act.

Responsible for Trudeau-mania, our stylish and popular prime minister had a reputation as a radical and a socialist. He was in reality very much a liberal, a democrat and a tireless advocate for positive change. He introduced divorce law reform and Criminal Code amendments liberalizing abortion laws, homosexuality and public lotteries. He also established a reputation as a defender of a strong federal government, to counter the separatist demands of Québec.

The War Measures Act gave the government extraordinary powers of detention, censorship and arrest. Shortly afterwards, Minister Laporte was murdered by the FLQ (Front de Liberation du Québec) terrorists. Was invoking the emergency war measures the right decision? The following statement, which Trudeau made the next year, sheds some light on his thinking:

"Recourse to violence is certainly the most disquieting phenomenon in modern society, and last October our democratic society was forced to limit the exercise of certain freedoms in order to defend itself against such violence. These limitations, no matter how short lived or slight, are intensely repugnant to the democrat. And so he asks himself how democratic freedom can be defended without denying its existence."[87]

In times of crisis, leaders must make difficult decisions, with no absolute certainty of a positive outcome.

Poverty is Not Insurmountable.

Born into poverty in the Appalachian Mountains, Carolyn Stradley and her brother lived in a hut, ate wild berries and trapped rabbits to stay alive. Her mother had died and her alcoholic father had abandoned the family. At 15, she found herself pregnant and began working as a secretary, while continuing her schooling. Happily married to the baby's father, they had started off well on their life plan, when he died unexpectedly. Now widowed, with a daughter to raise, she realized that she could make more money shoveling asphalt of the back of a pickup truck, than she could as an executive secretary.

She got a job doing exactly that. Fighting discrimination, workplace harassment and abuse, she pressed on, and studied engineering construction before starting a multimillion-dollar company, C&S paving, in Marietta, Georgia. Her company paved the track for the Olympic Stadium in Atlanta, and many other massive projects.[88]

> "Just when you think everything is gone. Look around and
> see what you've got left."
> Carolyn Stradley, CEO of C&S Paving

Financial Disaster or Freedom?

Can you really find fortune in ruins? A client relates the following story: "I tried everything, she said... the bank gave us a line of credit, we had a great location, and we had tons of clients and years of experience behind us. I had a great reputation, and thankfully, I still do. But, something was wrong with our plan. We were unrealistic about the amount of business we thought we could pull in. Our month-to-month carrying costs were killing us. After trying everything under the sun, and following the advice of some not so helpful people, I decided to give it up and downsize. I filed for bankruptcy. I cried and cried. Where I come from filing bankruptcy is a shameful thing to do. I was embarrassed to tell my family and I thought I would never get over it. I started over, and guess what? With a smaller operation, my income skyrocketed.

All our clients came back, and I did better financially than at any time before. Now we're planning an early retirement. I would not recommend bankruptcy to anybody, but I would recommend downsizing as soon as possible at any sign of trouble. And I would also recommend getting at least three opinions on any major financial decision."

In no way is financial disaster in the same category as some of the other catastrophes discussed in this chapter. For the person experiencing it, at least temporarily however, it does seem like the worst thing that could happen: for a small number of people, tragically, it is cause for suicide.

I am not a financial planner, and I am sharing the following common sense information with you so that you have some information to discuss with *your* financial experts, your spouse, your family. In order to get through financial crisis, (or to prevent one from occurring in the first place), these are some choices to think about:

1. Why do I/we want to purchase this? Is this purchase truly solving a problem, or meeting a need?

2. What are my values and goals around money? Am I willing to take on a second job to become financially secure? Am I willing to make the choices required, in order to enjoy more leisure hours at 65? 60? 55? Do I/we feel that it is our sole responsibility to provide for our children's education, or do we feel it is wise for them to generate some of their own income at the appropriate age?

3. Have we researched all of the issues and angles before making a purchase?

4. What can I/we sell, downsize, trade or barter, and stop doing, in order to maximize our available cash flow? What if we sold our house?

5. Should I spend this money right now, or can I save some cash instead?

6. There are two similar products for me to choose from. Can I walk away and come back later to make the best choice for me and my family?

7. If I absolutely need to purchase this product or service, can I do it with cash, or do I absolutely need to use credit?

8. If I absolutely have to use credit, how can I get the lowest interest rate, and pay it off as quickly as possible?

9. Have I looked at all of the benefits versus the true cost of making this purchase?

10. I'm being offered what looks like a good deal. What are the hidden costs, and whom can I speak with to compare the issues before making a decision to purchase?

It's all about *Freedom*. Financial security, or at least some basic monetary stability, is all about *Freedom*... the freedom to rest, the freedom to enjoy most of the activities you love throughout your life. No one says it better than financial wizard, Suzy Orman[89],

> 'A big part of financial freedom is having your heart and mind
> free from worry about the what-ifs of life."

Once again, remember... of all of the catastrophes one may encounter as they move through life on this planet, financial disaster is far from the most critical. If you have your health, and at least one good friend or/ and the love of at least one family member, you are wealthy, already. If you have, or can get access to resources to help you through the financial struggle, you are wealthy already. If you have the least ability to expand your financial base, through sideline businesses, or secondary income, you and your family are wealthy already. The choice is yours.

War

> "The mountaintop is the place of outlook over the earth and the sea. But it
> is in the valley of suffering, endurance, and self-sacrifice
> that the deepest visions of the meaning of life come to us."
> Henry Van Dyke [90]

One of the great dilemmas for proponents of positive psychology is the question, "But what about…?", where the seeker is reflecting on tornados, genocide, war, misogyny, the abuse of children in all its evil forms, and so on.

Though there may not be a definitive answer to this question, we do understand that there are many powerful laws and forces at work in the world. Contrary to a currently popular new age trend, I have always said that the law of attraction is *not* the only law dictating events as we see them. There are also the force of chaos, natural and created by man, and the force of evil itself, wearing all its seductive masks. Since time began, however, though millions of lives were lost along the way, good has always won over the powers of evil… eventually. And it will again.

The human race has gotten 'really good' at war. Finding issues to fight about, postage stamp size bits of land to kill each other over, and developing technology to do it on a grander scale, is truly one of humanity's greatest and most disturbing achievements. How can we possibly apply healthy thinking to the issue of war? The answer to that question lies in Malcolm Potts' and Thomas Haden's "Sex and War: How Biology Explains Warfare and Terrorism and Offers a Path to a Safer World."

Dr. Potts, who by the way is an obstetrician and research biologist, states the premise of the book, an in-depth study of war throughout history:

"Why do we humans, remarkably social animals with extremely large brains, spend so much energy on one thing… deliberately and systematically killing other members of our own species?" Malcolm Potts[91]

Potts and Haden outline the undeniable fact that warfare is decided upon, planned, generated, perpetrated and sustained by men. For anyone who may be unsure of this, look at gang murder throughout the world, or at people banding together on missions of genocide to torch villages and kill every living thing within it. Most violence, virtually all group violence, and certainly war, is a creation of the male of the species.

They also put forth a convincing argument that women are part of the solution. Economic development, family planning, and education of women are not just important factors in the liberation of women worldwide, they are elements usually accompanied by a drop in armed conflict.

Hailed by renowned experts working in the positive change movement such a Jane Goodall, Sex and War highlights how close human Behavior is to that of chimpanzees. Her comparison being that groups of young chimpanzee males raid other groups. They find the fittest females, hook up with them in classic Darwinian behavior, in the hopes of benefitting the next generation.

Sex and War offers a dose of realistic fact, and hope. For example:

- There was actually less warring going on in the 20th century than there was previously. Their research supports that most societies were at war, most of the time, before the 20th century.
- Rape as a weapon of war was much more common than it is now.
- The vast majority of people are actually not violent.
- Though biology and hormone levels do drive much of our behavior, and certainly, violence (testosterone), we do have the ability to make changes... we do have free will.

We need to think about, look for and *do* what makes peace.

With the litany of disturbing news about warfare and endless suffering in Iraq, Sri Lanka, Darfur, Afghanistan, Ethiopia, Somalia, and as the number of nuclear armed nations grows, it is important for world leaders to be focused on planetary survival by the means proposed by the Potts and Haden... by changing the very nature of *how we think*.

Out of great suffering as VanDyke says, emerges positive change, somewhere somehow, for the good of humanity. We are fortunate to live in a world where the megatrend of instant communication has placed evil under the microscope. It is by bringing light to evil that those crusading for good can, and will, succeed.

Good Does Triumph Over Evil

… just not always on our timetable. Here are three examples.

- The rising up of African-Americans and enslaved people, the downtrodden and the marginalized from lands the world over, against racism in all its forms, with the election of President Barack Obama proving that together, we *can* create positive change.
- The backlash and worldwide forces joining to fight the proliferation of child pornography, sexual abuse, and slavery of children.
- The refusal of the people to accept the continuing existence of the Berlin wall, ending in its astonishing and jubilant destruction.

There are times when some think our future is hopeless. It is vitally important during those times to turn our thoughts to events long past and recent, which prove the possibility of our triumphing over adversity and evil. Look to sources gathering factual good news from all over the world. Out of those stories, not only do you find comfort and hope, you and your community may find *one idea* that triggers a positive change project in your area.

Staying glued to 24-hour news of world disaster will not help us contribute to positive change. It will make us feel hopeless, depressed, and waste an amazing amount of time, which we could be using to help in some real way. It is important to be aware of news; however, knowing every single detail and watching it repeated over and over and over again, as some people spoke of during the 9/11 terrorism crisis, is counterproductive. Rather, doing something to help and moving from thought into action to help real people, such as joining or contributing to organizations like Free The Children[92] makes much more sense.

The top source I would recommend for reliable daily good news is the Good News Network[93], a news agency founded by Jerry Weis Corbley, a journalist by trade, who has devoted her life to the important work of the focus on all that is good and true in the news. The link is in the Endnotes.

Always Take a Parachute

"There are situations where, given the current circumstances, there is no
action or thought that, at this point, will make a
significant enough difference
to change the outcome that is barrelling down upon you."[94]
Esther Hicks

For those of you who know their work, it may astonish you that this quote comes from Esther and Jerry Hicks, the baffling and controversial absolute proponents of pure law of attraction theory. They share this statement, however, in the spirit of caring, for it is true that at some point, where catastrophe is crashing towards us, we may have little recourse. It is also true that save for those who would jump from a plane without a parachute, even in times of catastrophe, many will fare very well indeed. Survivors of imprisonment and torture often recount how they made it through the days, by *going within*, by going deep within their thoughts and *living inside their mind*. The parachute's threads are in your thoughts.

Perspective Exercise.

Learning to be more optimistic, sometimes dreaming of spectacular successes, and sometimes cautiously positive in the face of adversity, is a skill we can learn and improve. Try the following thinking exercise: how would you answer the question:

What common thread runs through the following stories?

<u>Roxana Saberi</u>, US-Iranian journalist, spent four months in an Iranian prison. She was wrongly convicted of spying, after a 15-minute closed-door trial. She reports that what gave her strength to survive the 100-day ordeal was singing the national anthem of the United States. [95]

<u>Between 1939 and 1945 an estimated 60 million people died</u> during the deadliest conflict in human history, World War II, including my uncle Gérard. He and my father enlisted, going to war to end the genocide of the Jewish people, and to prevent the annihilation of freedom the world over. My father came home. Gérard is buried in a wartime grave in Europe.

<u>A jet plane in a crash landing descent is brought safely down</u> into the Hudson River, and all 155 passengers escape safely. This type of disaster is typically fatal for all, from the crash itself or by drowning in the icy waters of the Hudson in this case.

<u>Rex Saunders, a 66-year-old fisherman, survived two long nights</u> on a chunk of ice near the northern edge of Newfoundland. His tiny boat had capsized. He was wearing a survival suit and kept singing a hymn while hoping to be rescued. He watched a helicopter circle a dozen times before they finally spotted him, after moving to the edge of the ice floe.[96]

What is the common thread in all the stories? No, it is not hymn singing, although singing is a common tactic reported by the survivors. It is that in times of trouble, all of these people went far *beyond* positive thinking. They all acted, and they acted on faith. They all *accepted* what was happening, and decided to *act* in the direction of positive change, ultimately overcoming adversity. They all drew from the well within themselves and found superhuman strength where many would have failed.

Healthy Thinking for Leaders

Whether you are a line supervisor, a department manager, a CEO, a teacher or a sports coach, your success will be enhanced in direct correlation with your ability to remain *realistically optimistic,* while maintaining your compassion for those who follow you. If this does not come naturally for you, try making some minor changes and shifts in your thinking and vocabulary:

- **Intent.** Begin each segment of your workday, morning, after a break, lunch or dinner with an optimistic, realistic inner thought exercise, which you have preplanned. Try this before a meeting, as one retired company president recently shared with me was one of his most effective success strategies throughout his entire career. Concentrate and bring to mind, your intent: tell yourself you will have a successful morning, afternoon or meeting, and that you will perform, and have enjoyable, effective interactions with everyone.

- **Better Vocabulary**. As you go about your day, evaluate and tweak your own words, vocabulary and phrasing. Feeling brave? Ask your executive assistant, one of your staff or colleagues to evaluate your conversation and point out any negative phrasing, discouraging commentary, sarcasm, or cynicism. Begin to replace negative vocabulary with healthier terms. An example would be, instead of saying, "We will have to hurry through this agenda. The safety inspector is here for a surprise audit," try, "We will work through the most important items on the agenda and make a plan for the next meeting. The safety inspector is here for a surprise audit. I'm glad I'm here to help." Do you notice the change in feeling with the second statement? What do you think your staff's reaction would be to each of those statements?

Dr. Wayne Dyer's acclaimed book, "The Power of Intention", has no competition in this arena. It is an in-depth study of the concept of intention and its application as a transformational tool. I highly recommend it. [97]

Helping Children through Catastrophe

Children react differently to catastrophe depending on their age, needs and previous experiences. Adults, parents and teachers, need to understand and know how to work with this reality. Every child is an individual. It is up to us to provide each child with the utmost in safety, emotional security, and reassurance.

We can help children talk through their feelings and understanding of catastrophe through play. With crayons and paper, you will see them draw out thoughts and feelings, arming us with more knowledge to help them. We can follow through by helping them understand that we are there for them.

If media are covering the disaster of the day, the best advice is to keep children away from horrific images. What do you think *they are thinking* as they watch? Children can be negatively affected by such images and easily develop patterns of nightmares and anxiety. This advice holds true for us as well. Is it necessary for to watch 12 hours of media coverage about a disaster? Or would we be better served by informing ourselves of the status of the situation, and then taking action in whatever way we can, small or large, in order to help the needy, ourselves our family, and to contribute to solutions?

Dandelion Children.

As parents, we naturally worry about the effect any troublesome events, let alone real catastrophe may have on our children. We fret about every parenting mistake we make, every time we have lost our temper, and every weakness and imperfection we displayed as role models. The truth is that amazingly, many children, some of whom have lived horrific experiences, some of whom have had very little of what we understand as *normal parenting,* fare extremely well and even go on to become high achievers and leaders in society. In Sweden, this phenomenon is called "dandelion children." In evidence throughout the world… this phenomenon is a testament to diversity in human adaptation and *our basic instinct to seek happiness.*

Dandelion children are so resilient they were given a label as a positive comparator to the flower we think of as a weed, one that will grow absolutely anywhere, in the toughest conditions. Just when you think it has been beaten down and could not possibly survive, there it is, popping up all over your lawn, up through the cracks in the pavement, no matter how harsh the environment. True, not all children are so resilient, and any focus on this phenomenon should not deter us from continuing our efforts to help and support those who are not dandelion children, but rather, more like delicate orchids, needing ongoing nurturing in order to succeed, perhaps on a lifelong basis, after trauma. Regardless of their ability to struggle or strive through disaster, every child is different and every child has value to the community and to society. Allowing disadvantaged children to remain invisible is to our detriment as a civilization. David Sloan Wilson, a researcher on childhood educations says it best:

"Such differences are valuable not just to individuals but to the culture as a whole, which profits from the diversity of interests and abilities." [98]

In my work, I frequently recommend exploring inspiring works from the worlds of the arts… "message" pieces, which help us gain knowledge and healthier perspectives on issues of concern, matters affecting us as individuals, families and groups. On the issue of abused, disadvantaged and marginalized children, I would recommend "Precious", the sensational film based on *Push*, a novel by the writer Sapphire.[99] A raw, disturbing, yet triumphant film, it is a story horrifically playing out in homes worldwide. Precious is film about an African American girl victimized by incest and struggling with obesity. At the end of the day, the message is that our Spirit, our Soul can triumph over the forces of evil. This film joins the battle raging against the epidemic of incest and sexual exploitation/abuse/rape of children, mostly girls, worldwide, now fueled further by the Internet.

Note: Always review the age rating for any film before letting children watch it. As well, for films including controversial issues, parents should view the film in its entirety before deciding if it is right for young children.

Communicating to Help the Child Affected by Disaster

Be prepared to answer your children's questions about the catastrophe. Your answers should be molded to fit the child's age and personality if possible. Start by asking the child, what she or he is thinking about. From there, ask them what questions *they* have. Avoid too much detail, adding more information only as they request it, and keep it simple.

Help the child to understand that we live on a planet that by nature has regular and irregular, often unpredictable, events that are chaotic. Help them learn about natural processes such as earthquakes and forest fires. These types of discussions are excellent opportunities for healthy dialogue with your child around issues of global responsibility. Even a young child can learn to understand that it is more difficult for those living in abject poverty to deal with catastrophe than it is for those of us who are more fortunate.

When a child asks a question such as "Could that happen here where we live?" your answer, once again depends on age. For a younger child, you may answer that you do not think so, that we all hope not, and that we are always preparing to be able to deal with trouble in our lives as a family and as a community. Always remember to reassure the child that we as adults are preparing to take care of them in such situations. For the older child, your answer would be similar, although perhaps with more detail and more healthy ideas about how they can keep themselves safe.

Even when children are affected by catastrophe, the healthy, caring, compassionate response of adults around them goes a long way to helping them in their current struggle, as well as in helping them prepare to be part of the positive change movement as they move through their life.

For an especially poignant example of a father protecting his small child from the horrors of war through brilliant communication, see the award-winning film, "It's a Beautiful Life," with Roberto Benigni. When he and his son are sent to a death camp, he convinces the child that it is all a game.[100]

Keep the following points in mind, in times of peace and well-being and review them in times of struggle:

1. Children will learn from all that we say and do not say in times of trouble. They will internalize our messaging, mimic it and carry it through life with them.

2. Our maintaining a calm demeanor and a reassuring presence is of utmost importance. Our children will learn this pattern, which will serve them well in the future.

3. Children need our knowledge and our ideas about our planet's realities and unpredictability. Natural and man-made disasters have always occurred, and will continue to happen, and children can understand that we are always learning to more successfully deal with these catastrophes.

4. Cultivating a compassionate, positive yet realistic approach to the management of catastrophe within families and communities increases our resiliency.

5. Be there, listen and show that you are thinking through what the child is saying, and always respond in a supportive way to their emotional needs

6. Help them to understand that family, friends and community organizations, are safe havens for them to go to in times of trouble.

7. Children can learn to meditate, pray, and use their imagination to create inner sanctuary for themselves if needed.

There are many more strategies that can be used to help children, the vulnerable elderly and people of all ages in times of catastrophe. There are groups in your area who are well trained and are training now for the management of crisis. These are groups that are often looking for volunteers, donations and help of every type in preparation and actual time of catastrophe. You may want to look to those groups when you find it possible to begin doing some volunteer work in your own life.

Got the Basics?

Do you have basic First Aid training? Do you know how to,

- Check for a pulse?
- Make sure an injured person can breathe air?
- Perform basic CPR? (Cardio Pulmonary Resuscitation)
- Stop a wound from bleeding?

Contact your country or area's heart and stroke organization, St. John's Ambulance[101], or other current sources, and get the basics. Print out basic how-to data sheets and keep them in your car, home and workplace. You will be glad you did one day.

Professional Disaster Relief Organizations

How can I help? Disaster relief is not "owned", by any one, or any individual or group or professional association. Disaster relief belongs to all of us. The more collaboration and integration of knowledge and resources exist within relief efforts, the higher the chances for success. Leaders must think differently than we have in the past.

The tragically slow and shamefully ineffective response to hurricane Katrina will remain forever in the history books, as the quintessential example of pathetic response to disaster relief. The "glass is ½ full" reality about Katrina is that an awakening emerged… to our need to think, communicate, and act differently, and to learn how to do it, *now.*

As an example, a new organization sprang up, post-Katrina, called RNRN. Never before had registered nurses banded together in such great numbers, and with this level of planning, to prepare for disaster. The first direct-care Registered Nurse national disaster network in the US, 4,200 volunteer RNs are now standing by, ready to relieve beleaguered colleagues in the next disaster zone."[102]

Most established and some newer organizations are listed with heartsandminds.org, a well-known source for helpful information. Their expertise is in motivating people to get involved and teaching how to make self-help, volunteering, and donations more effective. They work to reach people nationwide and globally through their excellent and highly useful website, public education and activism campaigns.[103] Hearts and Minds is a respected, effective agency, directed by a Board composed of members from a variety of occupations. Through their site, you could identify the organization you may be interested in exploring, to pitch in now or in the future.

Each individual has untapped power to make things better.
Hearts & Minds motto.

Notes:

Chapter 4

Heartbreak Syndrome

Well, since my baby left me,

I found a new place to dwell

It's down at the end of lonely street

At Heartbreak Hotel.

Lyrics from the Thomas Durden song, "Heartbreak Hotel,

made famous by Elvis Presley.[104]

There is no feeling like that of a heart broken by lost love. Infidelity or other betrayal by a partner, friend or family member, rejection based on race, sexual orientation or other differences... are all cause for heartbreak. In this chapter, however, we will focus on heartbreak based on the breakup of a romantic relationship. Breakup is common human experience, which, in our love-obsessed society, leads to dire consequences more often than it should.

Heartbreak Syndrome

Heartbreak is usually defined in terms of overwhelming grief, sorrow, deep sadness, or depression, and is triggered by the loss of someone deeply loved, either by death, or by the end of the relationship.

Initially, you may have feelings of confusion, panic, exhaustion, insomnia, oversleeping, nausea, anorexia, racing heartbeat, difficulty breathing, and emotional numbness. It is not uncommon to feel profound emotional pain, as well as physical pain, weight loss or weight gain. Feelings of bitterness towards the other person, and even towards the experience of life itself can emerge. Finding the energy to overcome the initial stages can seem like a monumental struggle. It can be as if we are paralyzed by the experience.

Going through the ups and downs of breakup is difficult, so much so, in fact, that we will even delay breaking up with someone when we know absolutely that it would be the best thing to do. We will resist having to face our own broken heart as long as possible. Regardless of whether we are the person triggering the breakup or our partner is, we will experience heartbreak syndrome to some degree.

Our soul longs so deeply for connection with another who truly loves us, that the loss of that connection can seem impossible to bear. Without some measure of healthy thinking, even the most successful of us will experience some risk to our own well-being at the time of a breakup. There is risk to our mental well-being when facing heartbreak without support.

Teen Heartbreak = Heartbreak

Adults have a tendency to negate adolescent heartbreak over lost love as inconsequential, a waste of energy, and not worthy of our attention. How wrong we are. For the teenager experiencing the pain of breakup, it is as excruciatingly painful as it would be for any adult. It is risky behavior to say the least, for the adults within any teenager's circle to ignore a breakup. Though everyone goes through heartbreak syndrome in their own way, the teenager experiencing breakup is at risk of depression, and making high-risk decisions.

Typical Scenario

Kim is an average student, attractive, with several close friends. She had been dating Trevor, the love of her life, for six months. She dreamed of their future together, where they would go to University, the city they would move to, the home they would buy, the two perfect children they would have, the vacations they would take together… the happy life they would enjoy.

Kim had her first sexual experience, with Trevor, at fifteen. They had been having frequent sex, including intercourse, for three months. One day, in the school cafeteria, Trevor tearfully told her that though he still cared deeply for her, he wanted to date other girls, and broke up with Kim. He was very kind and gentle with his words and wished her well, telling her that if she ever needed anything he would be there for her.

Kim experienced feelings of shock, numbness, and even heard herself saying to Trevor, "No! Can't we just try again? Maybe if we took a little time apart… "

After he left, she went home in a trance-like state, went to her room, and stayed there until the next day. She did not tell her family of her sorrow, and cried herself to sleep. Kim continued to feel depressed, and even began to feel that her life was without meaning. She felt that no one would ever love her. Feeling betrayed, she thought that the special love she and Trevor had was ruined and falsely based. She had thoughts of cutting herself, and even suicide.

Kim's friend Allison was the first to hear the news, as Kim poured her heart out to her for hours. The next day, Allison went home with Kim after school and was with her when Kim finally told her mother. Her family and friends rallied to support her through this and were there for her in her darkest times. She had many ups and downs over a period of three months.

Slowly, her mood began to lift until one day, for the first time, Kim laughed out loud. She was watching a movie with Allison, and literally could not stop laughing. She had experienced a breakthrough, and knew she was now able to move forward.

Avoid Isolation

To anyone experiencing breakup or heartbreak of any kind: *avoid isolation.* Seek out counsellors, a health or social service professional you trust, your closest family members and friends… the ones who typically make good decisions. Avoid the ones who want you to do drugs or get drunk to get through this. Avoid the urge to have sex with someone just "to show him", or to have sex with as many people as possible, to numb the pain.

An Open Door

To adults within the life circle of the teenager experiencing breakup, now is the time to clearly offer an open door, and a non-judgemental ear. And, no, your teen does not need your 'relationship advice' right now.

Am I Worthless?

The pain felt during relationship breakup is largely caused by a diminished sense of worth. It is important for us to rebuild good feelings about ourselves. The following are some typical questions and thoughts we have following breakup.

- Am I worthless? Why do others have a boyfriend / girlfriend, and I don't?
- How will I survive this failure?
- Will I ever find someone?
- What if he/she wants me back? Should I hope for that?
- I feel like a part of me is missing. Will that feeling ever go away?
- I am the one who broke the relationship up. Did I do the right thing?
- Why can't I stop thinking about him/her?

Be Selective

The most nurturing thing you can do for yourself at this time is to be selective about what you dwell on. When you find your mind going around in circles, thinking about the same painful thoughts over and over again, it is time to turn the switch off.

- Forgive yourself, for anything you could possibly think you may have done "wrong" in the relationship. Focus on any positive aspect about yourself instead, the moment self-deprecating thoughts creep in.

- Seek out and spend time with a trusted person you know. This could be a health or social services professional, who will honestly acknowledge the pain you are feeling and help support you through this time. What *you do not need to hear* is "Don't worry; everything is going to be all right. You'll meet somebody else."

- Spend time thinking about the positive aspects of "You". It might help for you to do so by writing down answers to the following questions:

1. Who do I know who enjoys spending time with me?

2. Whose life is made better because of knowing me?

3. Who do I help occasionally or on a regular basis?

4. What have I been successful at?

5. What talent or talents, do I have?

6. When I am in a group, what positive influence do I have on my team members?

7. What were the last three compliments someone gave me?

- Remember that all troubles eventually pass.

- Acknowledge the fact that heartbreak is common, and for most people, this includes breakup at some point in their lives. Think about the fact that after a varying period of time, for all of these people, the heartbreak ends, and better times do come.

- Do some research around the well-known fact that many people find once the pain of heartbreak is over and life goes on, the best thing that could have happened to them, relationship wise, was the breakup.

- During moments where the heartbreak feels especially bad, (remember that this can come and go), do some simple breathing exercises. Simply breathe in for three seconds then breathe out for three seconds. Repeat two or three times. Try to let go of the bad feeling by thinking, or saying out loud, "I know that I can feel better again. I know that I will feel better again… maybe even right now."

- Choose an uplifting song as your theme through your healing period. Listen to it as often as it takes to return to a good feeling place within you.

- Only watch movies and documentaries that present good outcomes after troubled times. There are many websites dedicated to providing you with lists of inspirational movies. During your grieving period, make sure to avoid movies, books, and music with dark, frightening, evil themes or terrible endings. In fact, avoid these from now on.

- Create a scrapbook about all of the positive aspects in your life… past, present, as well as goals and dreams for your future. Being visually reminded of past good times gives us a boost of endorphins.

- Build your support team of caring individuals and supportive people including professionals, and keep their contact information handy so you always have someone to turn to.

- Most importantly, if you are having suicidal thoughts, seek out a mental health professional or agency, your nurse practitioner, physician, or dial 911 immediately.

The Support Person

Are you the support person this time? It may also be necessary for you to bring the person to counselling. Family counselling center personnel, mental health professionals and hospital emergency staff are trained to assess and help the individual unable to cope with the shock and potential depression related to heartbreak. When in doubt, it is always better to seek an assessment than to avoid it for fear of a long wait in a waiting room or uncomfortable questioning.

Recent loss of a loved one, regardless of the circumstances, is a well-known contributing factor to depression and even suicide[105]. This is true, regardless of age… 18 or 88, it is of concern. Though this chapter focused on the example of a teenage girl, even the elderly can experience heartbreak syndrome.

Positive Aspects about Experiencing Love, Permanent or Not

Heartbreak is an emotional, spiritual injury. As we heal, we tend to acknowledge more and more of the positive aspects about having been in the relationship, now being out of it, and about what the relationship helped us learn. From every love relationship in our lives, whether it is romantic love, parent-child love, friendship love, temporary loves and lasting ones, we are able to draw on the experience. The voice of wisdom speaks to us. We are maturing. We are learning to think differently about the experience. Some people find listing the positive aspects, in writing, very helpful. You may even have a few laughs along the way. Some examples include planning not to repeat the same mistakes, or having become wiser. We certainly become stronger individuals through the experience of failed relationships and can help others through similar experiences.

Find Your Own Path to Renewed Joy

Explore putting into play some of the ideas and strategies that struck a chord with you in this chapter. Do so while spending quality time with your friends and family. Try getting involved in at least one new activity. Explore your creative side. Keep yourself busy. Attend a concert. Treat yourself to something you enjoy *at least once a week*. A massage from a registered massage therapist maybe? An uplifting movie at the mulitplex? Remember, you do not need to be with someone else at all times and in fact, it can be therapeutic to do something new like going to an activity on your own once you are over the initial trauma.

This may not feel like the time to read some positive psychology. Your energy is low, you might even feel like sleeping a lot of the time, or you might not be interested in reading or reviewing any self-help material. Find some anyway, created by someone you can relate to. Sometimes, we just *have to do what we have to do*. Ask yourself:

"Do I really want to maintain this lonely, depressed feeling for much longer?

This is the perfect time to look into new and better thinking strategies. I guarantee you that once you find someone's work you can relate to, you will be motivated to explore. Maybe you are more comfortable with a professional positive psychology source such as the University of Pennsylvania's Dr.Martin Seligman and his Authentic Happiness website. You can develop personal insights through the secure, scientifically tested questionnaires, for starters.[106] The Sedona Method[107], a *letting go* strategy, is also highly recommended and endorsed by professionals from the helping field

Your "I Deserve This" List

When you feel ready to start exploring new friendships, meeting new people and perhaps one day finding a partner to share your life with, in my experience the healthiest thinking strategy for you to adopt is around your *focus*. Focus on attracting the type of person who makes you *feel good about yourself*, who respects you, who is faithful, and who always has your best interests at heart.

Making lists of the physical qualities your partner should have, the amount of money they make, the type of clothes they need to be wearing, where they come from, what type of work they do, and all of those types of characteristics, are a waste of your time. The key to joy in relationships is to be with *people who really care about you…* who you can laugh with, cry with and who love you with no makeup on. They love you even if your muscles are not what they were at 25. They are interested in what you are doing and they will be there when you are sick, not at your best, and they will hang in there through the tough times. Why would you settle for anything less?

Clarity through Contrast

Gaining clarity about any decision you are trying to make, is easier to achieve if you know exactly what you would like. Make a contrast list to simplify this. This will help you clarify the types of situations you are looking to attract, and the types of events, people, things and experiences that would bring you joy. The strategy is simple.

Regardless of what the issue is, and in this case we are talking about getting through heartbreak, create a list on a sheet of paper. Draw a line right down the middle. On the left-hand side, title the list, "What I *don't* want." On the right-hand side, title the list "What I *do* want." Now begin listing everything you do *not* want in your next relationship. Everything. All the things that made you feel bad in this relationship you have just come out of. Once you have exhausted all possible aspects, take a deep breath. Now go to the right side. Start listing all of the *things you do want* in the next relationship, in a permanent relationship, if you are at that stage of your life. If you are 'stuck' on the right side, simply begin writing the exact opposite of what is on the left side. For example, if you wrote on the left side. "Criticizes my clothing." (you don't want that), on the right side, you could write, "Compliments what I wear." And so on. You will probably find that all kinds of new ideas will spring up and generate feelings of pleasure and hope, as you create *your* list of things you *do* want in your new relationship. With that in mind, go for it!

Whether it is meditation, law of attraction strategies[108], prayer, or joining a self-help group, you have a right to practice and enjoy whatever method helps you through this. You have every reason to confidently seek out strategies, old and new, as well as the counsel of others who have been there, survived and thrived. There is something out there that will help pull you out of heartbreak syndrome.

> "...... everything on the earth has a purpose,
> every disease an herb to cure it,
> and every person a mission.
> This is the Indian theory of existence."
> Mourning Dove Salish, 1888-1936

Notes:

Chapter 5

Workplace Challenges

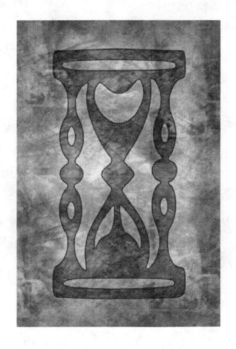

Go to the people, live among them. Learn from them. Love them.

Start with what they know, build on what they have.

But of the best leaders, when their task is accomplished, and their work is done,

the people will remark, "we have done it ourselves."

Ancient Eastern Saying

"Mr. Jones, we no longer need your services"

It may seem strange to start a chapter on work life wellness with a statement like that one. Any one who has had the often heart-wrenching task of saying those words to an employee, knows how difficult this is. The strange thing is, several people who were terminated from employment have told me it turned out to have been one of the best things that happened in their careers.

For the vast majority of employers, having to fire someone is a difficult and long thought out process, and truly it is a last resort. In all probability, if you are being terminated, your boss has consulted with human resources experts, and almost certainly obtained legal counsel or the advice of human resource experts before moving forward. It is not done callously, as there is always a risk to the agency, should the decision be wrongly based. Here are some real-people examples of eventual life outcomes, post-termination:

- A service professional, fired after over twenty-five years of dedicated service to one employer, realized she no longer needed that level of income. She and her husband have begun traveling. They are now both planning early retirement. She decided to not return to the workplace, in pursuit of personal interests and hobbies instead.

- A young department manager in a midsized organization thanked his supervisor for the termination as they shook hands before he left the office. He commented about how he had enjoyed working there, that he knew it was coming, and that he appreciated the support he had gotten along the way. He now runs his own successful business.

- Knowing in her heart that she was about to be terminated, a worker with over ten years experience resigned voluntarily and was successful in obtaining a more satisfying, more lucrative management position with a larger organization.

Being laid off, fired or terminated can happen to anyone. The reasons are many, and often related to necessary changes in the structure of the organization, or to company financial issues. Though it may not feel like it initially, this is a time when you are truly a position to Turn Crisis Into Opportunity ©.[109]

You are not alone. Hundreds of thousands of people are terminated in North America every year. Know that you may go through a period of embarrassment, resentment, and may even feel elements of grief.

What Do I Do Next?

- Forgive yourself for anything you may have done to contribute to the termination. It is over. Done. In the past. You cannot change it now. Be kind to yourself, and avoid dwelling on the event.

- Avoid any magical thinking that the phone will ring and you will be offered your old job back.

- Use your frustration, anger and bewilderment energies to begin creating a plan for finding a new and perhaps better position, starting a business, or both.

- Consider visiting an employment consultant, or seek legal counsel, if you feel you were wrongly terminated. These experts can also help you determine if in fact, you have received all compensation owed to you. Your area may have a non-profit employment center, and many lawyers do not charge for the first visit.

- Revise your resume and cover letters. Focus on the basics, and make sure that your cover letter addresses the actual job you are applying for. Include solid reasons why you qualify for this position. There is no need to bring in the subject of your firing. Potential employers can read between the lines and may suspect you were fired, yet call you in for an interview regardless, based on your qualifications. They know that not everyone can function perfectly in every possible position, and they may think you have high potential to do well with them.

- Review all of your answers against your resume and make sure you are consistent and not contradicting yourself.
- Be honest in answering questions on job application forms, and use terms such as "position no longer required" or "terminated". If at any time in written or verbal communications, you are asked if you were fired, answer "yes". Lying in a job application process is grounds for dismissal later on.

You Have an Interview!

Have you thought of volunteering that you were fired? Sounds counter-intuitive, doesn't it? In the interview, some experts recommend volunteering that you were terminated instead of waiting for anybody to ask. [110] You can then explain the reasons in a positive light. If you were fired because of something you did, you can briefly talk about the lessons you learned, and how you are even more prepared to be an excellent employee at this time. Whether you decide to volunteer the news or not, here are some ideas (if they are true for you) to help develop your own answers to the delightful question, "Why were you fired?"

- "They never gave a reason. Though I didn't think so at the time, it turned out to be one of the best things that happened to me. I'm able now to look for a position that's better suited to my qualifications and skills."
- "I usually get along very well with my supervisors, but this time, we just didn't click. I really can't pinpoint all the personal reasons."
- "I've thought a lot about why I left, and I know that I did make some mistakes. Now I see it at as a learning experience, and I'm looking forward to proving how I've grown with a new employer."
- "I ended up working for a new boss, and she did a lot of restructuring. I was downsized."

Make sure that the answers you prepare are honest and that you are comfortable speaking the words. Practice answering the toughest questions. Better yet, videotape yourself. Have some fun with it, and ask a friend to play the role of the interview panel.

Make sure that nothing you are posting to the Internet can negatively affect your job prospects in any way. Google yourself once in awhile to see if anybody else has posted anything negative or false about you. Have it taken down if that is the case. It is your right.

Think Workplace Wellness

- Remember that you deserve healthy workplace experiences and a good work life.
- Think through and visualize yourself having the experience of a successful job interview. Create a written script about how this will play out, and practice it in your mind, just as all professional athletes are taught to.
- Create a vision board specifically loaded with images of successfully landing a new and even better position. Include your smiling face in the images even if it means you need to cut out and superimpose it onto those you may find in magazines.
- Enjoy the free time in between positions, and make the best of it with fun activities and reconnecting with old friends and family.
- Take advantage of the necessary belt-tightening in between jobs, to start new, thriftier, environmentally supportive practices, and perhaps even to downsize your living quarters, and vehicle.
- Always speak calmly, in a neutral manner, in positive language about your previous employer and workplace.

When Scrooge Becomes Mary Poppins

Nothing will create more cynicism and suspicion amongst employees, than a previously grumpy manager suddenly becoming Mary Poppins. In times of trouble, however, anyone in a supervisory capacity knows and feels deep down that those who look to you for leadership need some realistic optimism. If you are not genuine, regardless of what buzzwords you are using, *they simply will not buy it.*

"The BS meter just goes Ding Ding Ding Ding Ding! People pick up on that." Says Gerard Seijts, a professor of organizational behavior at the Richard Ivey school of business at the University of Western Ontario. [111]

One of the greatest secrets to enjoying your work, and helping others in your workplace enjoy theirs, is for you to Be Your Self. Intertwined with the skills you use, the tasks you were assigned, and the day-to-day activities and events in your workplace, there is always a way for you to be your self, while performing in a professional and competent manner. Clients love it. Colleagues love it. And the more you learn to be yourself in the workplace, the more you will... yes... Love Your Job.

The Optimist's Club

"In this world, the optimists have it, not because they are always right, but because they are positive. Even when they are wrong, they are positive, and that is the way of achievement, correction, improvement, and success. Educated, eyes open, optimism pays."

David Landes, on The Wealth and Poverty of Nations [112]

Think of the Dalai Lama or President Barack Obama. Being optimistic does not guarantee that you're going to live a life free of difficulties. We all know there is no such thing. There are many forces at work in the universe, not all of them positive. The greatest leaders tend to be optimistic.

How do I Lead "Consciously?"

Conscious leaders understand and accept the responsibility they have towards global positive change. By implementing ethical best practices, their current work is aligned with the positive change movement, almost by default. Conscious leadership has, as one of its core values, realistic effective optimism. Not as complicated as it sounds, it is all about learning, developing, nurturing, and applying healthy thought processes in our leadership work. Effective positive vocabulary follows, and from that, positive change through action.

Dysfunctional workplaces always have strong negative forces at work within, inherently influencing certain employees. For the most part, individuals are not consciously intending to 'be a negative influence,' though sometimes that is the case, and it is up to the effective leader to resolve the situation. If the employee fully realized the impact of their actions on their colleagues, their clients and *their own health*, they would in most probability, make other choices. It is fascinating to observe the power that these individuals sometimes have. Whether in the front lines or tucked away in cubicles, they can develop a following of easily influenced colleagues, who for various reasons, are falling in step with the dysfunctional behavior. One of the reasons this following develops is that staff is starved for leadership.

A dysfunctional workplace will only become truly well again when those negative forces are transformed for the good of all, or... move on to someone else's employ. They themselves may actually be much happier and more effective in a new place of employment. One such individual, who is much happier in his new employ, said to me. "I don't know why I stayed there so long. I love it here." He is a positive force in his new workplace, something his previous employer and colleagues would find astonishing.

The conscious leadership movement is experiencing significant growth in the academic and research field. Positive organizational development is not just pie in the sky anymore; potential employees are actually looking for organizations where the culture has these elements, where 'the bosses' work on making 'this a great place to work', and where leaders think differently. Here are some ideas for conscious leadership and some excellent resources.

Appreciative Inquiry.

Developed in the 1980s by David Cooperrider, and now in practice worldwide, Appreciative Inquiry is a simple, highly effective strategy for approaching problems and planning.[113] It boils down to thinking differently, and using four basic steps in any situation. It can be used in brainstorming sessions, monthly meetings or even as a solitary exercise in planning, and ideally as an organizational philosophy, or "It's the way we do things around here." For organizations and groups, it is a great model to use during troubled times. The steps are:

1. **Discovery**

    List "the best of What Is", pertaining to the issue at hand. Do so in the spirit of focus on the most positive facts about the current situation while acknowledging and valuing the past. Honouring the past emphasizes the value of that work. Looking at achievements, financial assets, core competencies and opportunities nurtures positive change. I would suggest in a brainstorming exercise, that a facilitator carve out a maximum of 20% of the time for focus on problems of the past, with 80% of the time focusing on the best part of "What is" now.

2. **Dream**

    Next is the fun part. Spend time brainstorming "What might be". Let the imagination soar. Have some fun with this part of it. Keep going until the group has exhausted all potential ideas no matter how far-fetched they may be. I recommend the use of diagrams, circles, square and triangles to frame brainstorming notes. Images and visual aids help to generate new thinking.

3. **Design**

What *should* be?" The third step is to make choices for positive change. This is where all involved plan new ways of doing things, re-create and transform, launch pilot projects and generally stir things up a little. Through this process, everything going on in the system or organization starts to align and truly gel towards the Dream.

4. **Destiny**

In this final an ongoing stage of appreciative inquiry, the entire organization is working with inspired action. Learning and innovation are supported. Employees are encouraged to continue ongoing dialogue with management in an effort towards continuous positive change.

Take This Job and Love It!

"In spite of the long office hours, I am thoroughly enjoying my career at KPMG. For me, being busy is a positive sign. It means I profit from the rapid pace of personal development as it boosts the overall thinking process and acquisition of soft skills." Ricci Chan

What is with this Mr. Chan, and how would he react to a real crisis in his work life?[114] Probably very well indeed. People who do what they love, and love what they do share basic characteristics. Here are a few:

- They are more motivated and happy when they can perform in a way that is natural *to them.*
- They make themselves understood by their colleagues and supervisors. No one has to guess what they are all about. They are clear communicators.

- They understand and value others' differences.
- They have good or even high levels of energy, and like being busy. They will look for more work if they are 'done' first.
- They love to learn and are continuously improving their skills.
- In crisis, they emerge as leaders.

It would not hurt to keep the last bullet tucked away for the next workplace crisis.

The more you nurture your own love of your work, the more you are able to get through tough times in the workplace, career glitches, terminations, re-locations, lay-offs, downsizing… and help lead or role model when crisis strikes. There is nothing like the sound of these words, when all hell is breaking loose at work:

"How can I help?"

Notice that the question is *not*,

"Let me know if I can help. I'll be in my office," or the not-so-helpful,

"If you need anything, you know where to find me."

"'How can I help," is a very specific question, seeking to determine the exact thing that the person needs at that moment. I remember being in charge during a particularly challenging time several years ago. One day, a front line employee stopped me in the hallway, commented on having heard about "The Trouble," and offered to help in any way required, even if it meant extra work or travel. Just knowing there was that team spirit, alive and well, and that someone I hardly knew was willing to step out of the comfort zone and offer help, made all the difference in the world that day – that week!

Of key significance is the fact that employees like that one truly love their work. They are great in a crisis, and are the foundation of functional workplaces.

Confronted by a 'Difficult Person'?

(… and sometimes the difficult person is us!)

"People don't resist change. They resist being changed!"

Peter Senge, Learning Organization expert [115]

Have you ever been in a work situation where you dreaded going in, knowing you had to work with someone you were having trouble with? We have all been there, and for those of you just entering the work force, you have probably experienced it in your academic life. Please note that the following strategies are just some of the ones I have found helpful,   at times fairly quickly. This information is in no way exhaustive, however it should launch you in the right direction, and provide you with some ideas to discuss with your human resource staff or manager.

Who is the Difficult Person?

First, let's stop, think objectively and look at what's really going on for that person you dread seeing. Rare is the person who consciously wants to be difficult…

- He may be unaware of his Behavior and effect on others.
- She does not realize how damaging her actions are to her own career and personal success.
- He is operating from the negative side of his personality.
- She may have developed negative Behavior habits due to work or personal stress, mental health issues, sexual, physical or mental abuse, and a myriad of other reasons. No baby comes into this world planning to be miserable.

Key Facts
- We will frequently work alongside others who may challenge us, and even challenge our ability to complete work assigned to us.

- Taking the time to think differently, trying to understand the other's viewpoint is highly valuable.

- Changing our attitude toward them and changing our perception about what makes them "wrong" can give us knowledge, which will contribute to our own ability to work with people.

- Occasionally, we find ourselves in situations where "we + they" is not a 'match', and never will be. All parties have options to deal with this scenario.

However, if the person in question is truly a 'bully', their goal may be to get *you* to leave, and maintain a workplace environment where they control all others. The conscious leader applies attention to this issue, and works on resolving it, for the good of all employees, the organization, and ultimately, the client it serves.

A Sampler of Difficult People "Types". *There are many.*

A. The String

You can't push a string. This person has Passive-Aggressive personality disorder. Seemingly quiet and unassuming, this person is in fact, a master of control. Using procrastination, stubbornness, and an outwardly weak persona, he or she resists, obstructs and sabotages change to anything that disturbs a carefully set up status quo. Surprised when confronted, the response is more passivity and sabotage. The String is often in reality, the most powerful member of their team.

B. Mr. or Miss "The Sky Is Falling!"

What I also call the "Gloomer Doomer", this person is whiny, fearful, negative, and sees the cup as half-empty. If something good happens, he or she may comment, "Don't get too excited. It's not going to last."

C. **The Wet Blanket**

The wet blanket makes it his or her job to point out all that is wrong with just about anything anyone comes up with.

D. **Mrs. or Mr. "I'm No Good At That. You Do It"**

This person has many tried and true strategies to get out of work and responsibility. They include seeking out the least confident or newest employees to pass work onto them.

E. **The Bully**

The Bully's goals are to control, gain special treatment and eliminate stronger, threatening forces. If the Bully has been in the workplace for a long enough period time, he or she may have amassed a remarkable amount of control over many aspects of the functioning of the organization, regardless of their position within the organizational hierarchy. "I get my way or, somebody pays." The Bully's greatest fear? Losing control.

F. **The Know-It-All**

Don't dare to question the Know-It-All. If you share a fact you just learned about, not only does the Know-It-All already know it, he or she knows a lot more about it than you do, and always will. The arrogance displayed is a defense against vulnerability and insecurity. The Know-It-All's Greatest fear? Losing credibility and respect.

Results of Difficult People's Behavior

1. Others eventually refuse to deal with them, or even work with them, unless they absolutely have to.

2. *Note to leaders*: Some of *your best employees may leave* if the issue is not resolved. If not dealt with, the difficult employee may have succeeded in diminishing management's respect and credibility.

3. People do not believe them, and generally mistrust them.

4. A general attitude may develop within the organization that the individual is not as competent as they profess to be.

5. They are often fired.

6. Others avoid telling them the truth or providing them with vital information.

7. Colleagues ignore their opinions or decisions.

8. Coworkers and supervisors will avoid implementing their ideas.

9. Subordinates will learn to subvert their authority (consciously or unconsciously).

10. They live a life of stress, internal and external, have health issues and miss finding joy in their life's work.

11. They are often sick.

Think and Succeed with Difficult People

Review the following strategies, pick one or two and practice them, maybe out loud, with a friend or in front of a mirror, as if they were actually happening to you. This guarantees your daily laugh out loud (actually, you should have three LOLs daily). Play them out in mental visual exercises, which generate a positive feeling for you, in the role your workplace requires you to play. Think about yourself in actual situations and picture it in your mind as if played out *with an excellent result*.

1. When someone verbally attacks you, stop, remain calm. Just observe, and move on. Review your workplace policy for harassment and

follow through, as appropriate. The goal is for you to maintain good feelings about your performance, your workplace life (Which is how many hours per month?) That person may be miserable, but you want to love your job.

2. With an irate client, breathe calmly and regularly through the incident. Bring back some of your favorite thought statements such as "Somehow, this is all going to work out." Take in what they have to say – take notes if appropriate, and let them know that you want to ensure their satisfaction if possible. Ask if you can have someone else participate in the discussion. If you made a mistake, follow your company policy – (common policy elements to look for: Do I apologize or not? Do I seek a resolution? How?). If the person is verbally abusing you, tell them you realize they are upset, and that you need to withdraw from the conversation until they can speak to you in a respectful manner. You may state that you feel threatened by them, and end the scenario abruptly if necessary. Speak with your supervisor as soon as possible and document all that you can remember about the incident. As soon as possible, practice a favorite mental exercise to return yourself to a calm pleasant state. Take a walk in a pleasant setting if possible during your break. Avoid rehashing the incident over and over, and refocus on thoughts and images that trigger better feelings within you, feelings of competence and enjoyment of your work.

3. Realize that the person is feeling very insecure, angry, defensive, taken advantage of, may have a permanent personality disorder, or be having mental health symptoms at that time.

4. Avoid pushing them to accept any particular solution.

5. Remain positive and professional in your vocabulary and body language. Be confident, empathetic and pleasant.

What if the Difficult Person is my Boss?

If the difficult person is your boss, and you have tried all possible strategies to improve your workplace situation, and you continue to be miserable, highly stressed and unhappy, think about what this is doing to your health, your relationships and your life path. This is a time for you to consciously *lead yourself.*

Talk to someone who has been through this type of situation. There may be a human resource organization in your area, and you can certainly seek this type of information online, from reliable well-established organizations involved in workplace wellness. Your public health organization may also have helpful resources, information, or even workshops that in some way can help you through this time, and actually help you make the right decisions. Reconsider whether it is time to find a job elsewhere. Maybe this one is no longer *a match*.

Supervising People who are Positively Challenged?

Even in times of workplace upheaval, downsizing and restructuring, for leaders, the ongoing development of a positive workplace culture is not only expected, in this day and age, it is part of our responsibility. Conscious leadership is choosing to be courageous, and to do what needs to be done. In my role as executive leader of a healthcare organization, on the first day of taking on the daunting responsibilities ahead of me, I wrote out on a small piece of paper,

"Do the tough stuff first."

I kept it in my desk and over the years it was a reminder to do exactly that. This does not mean things automatically fall into place 100% of the time, but you will be pleased at how much clearer your thinking is, how much easier it can be to make good decisions, when you tackle the most difficult situations first.

For the most part, it is challenging to work with commitment, creativity and compassion while trying to deal with difficult people on your team. However, there is a real possibility of awakening the difficult person to their true nature. You might be able to help them tap into their own source of inspiration, triggering behavior change, and even releasing talents and abilities they have not used yet. How?

1. Help them see how much their negative behavior is damaging their career potential, as well as their workplace relationships. You may need advice from your human resource expert to help you think through the best approach and explore the possible choices for working with the person.

2. Help the person set time-sensitive goals aimed at learning to work more collaboratively with others. Monitor their behavior and clearly, meaningfully acknowledge all improvement.

3. If the Behavior does not improve within a reasonable time, effective leadership demands that some movement forward, for the good of all concerned, especially the client, must take place. If this includes helping an unhappy destructive employee find a more suitable employment area, than that positive change is what must be.

Note to employers: It can take up to one full calendar year for the organization to heal and recover after the departure of a long-time-in-power difficult employee.

Yikes! I'm in Trouble at Work.

If negative is how *you* are most of the time, it is seriously affecting all aspects of your life. How will you tackle larger life problems and crisis? Do yourself a favor... Get a grip on this now. Choose to work on at least two of these elements, and see the difference it makes in your day-to-day enjoyment of your work.

1. Pay attention to situations where you become defensive: realize that you are probably not really being attacked. Practice reacting more slowly, calmly, being more open to the other person's perspective.

2. Learn and practice enjoyable thought and visualization techniques, including scenarios of yourself being positive, happy, fulfilled, liked… at work.

3. Practice attentive listening when someone asks a question or makes a suggestion. Ask the person to re-state their question or suggestion if you need to. Try to understand what others are saying by repeating back *what you think you heard*. Why not ask for more time to respond, and then get back to them if appropriate? Research listening skills and tips. Try one at a time.

4. Find someone who can help you work on your negative aspects. Offer to help them with something in return. If your helper is someone you interact with regularly, be brave. Ask them to alert you when you are being difficult. Learn to see what situations and events trigger your Behavior.

Changing negative habits begins with changing the underlying thinking creating the behavior. It can take months or years of work, and it *is* worth it. Stay with it. Acknowledge and celebrate the significant positive changes you will create in your own life. Use this period of self-improvement to explore and understand your own personality, strengths and weaknesses. Your effort will be rewarded as you find more career opportunities opening up, more joy in your life, and a strengthened ability to handle crisis.

Success at Work – In Good Times and in Bad

Robin Sharma, in his storybook style bestseller, "Leadership Wisdom from the Monk who Sold his Ferrari", bases his advice on a series of time proven strategies successful leaders are known for.[116] Though some "old guard" leaders pooh-pooh them, and desperately try to hang on to 19th century management practices, Sharma and many other superstars of leadership in the world today teach variations of similar themes.

He spoke to my colleagues and I in an executive forum a number of years ago. Many of us were grappling with complex organizational issues, financial decisions in the six and seven figures, and as always at these types of events, leaders are listening for inspiration they can use... *now*. The simplicity of what he said struck me. For true meaning and success in our work, regardless of whether we are in the corner office or on the assembly line, in the welding shop, the hair salon, in good times and in bad, some basics will always be true. Some of them are as simple as learning, and *actually applying*, with as much expertise as possible, basic effective communication skills. Some of them are simple habits your mother probably taught you, such as "Get up early, get more done." And one of the most essential, especially when things are very difficult in your work life, is that we must find the *meaning* in what we do.

In all probability, going to work from one day to the next has meaning for us that sits somewhere along the continuum of going to work "because:

1. I have to, and I despise every moment of it."

2. It's what I do, and it's okay I guess."

3. I have chosen this work. I'm pretty good at it, but I'd rather work somewhere else."

4. I have learned what I needed to know to be highly competent at this. I enjoy going in most days."

5. I have worked long enough to be really good at what I do. I've taught a lot of people along the way, and it's time for me to relax."

6. I love what I do. I would even be doing this, or some form of it, if no one paid me for it. When I'm working, I get lost in what I do, and lose all track of time."

We sometimes find the deepest meaning when the most difficult of crises occur. Should you find yourself in such a situation now or in the future, give yourself permission to reflect on all that has happened, and find meaning for you. Acknowledge your part in helping others, and in doing your job as best as you possibly could, under the circumstances.

Inspiration for the Workplace

The following poem has been widely mis-attributed to Ralph Waldo Emerson, and others, often as a quote. It was actually written by Betty Anderson Stanley, an American woman who wrote it for an essay contest in 1904. It really is a gem of healthy thinking. Enjoy.

Success

He has achieved success
who has lived well,
laughed often, and loved much;
who has enjoyed the trust of
pure women,

the respect of intelligent men and
the love of little children;

who has filled his niche and accomplished his task;

who has left the world better than he found it
whether by an improved poppy,
a perfect poem or a rescued soul;

who has never lacked appreciation of Earth's beauty
or failed to express it;

who has always looked for the best in others and
given them the best he had;

whose life was an inspiration;
whose memory a benediction.

1904 Bessie Anderson Stanley[117]

Gisèle Guénard

Notes:

Chapter 6

Caregiver Burnout

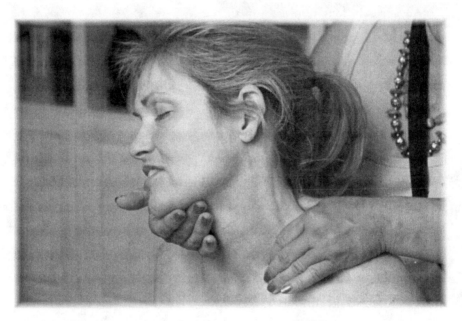

How important it is for us to recognize and celebrate our

heroes and she-roes!

Maya Angelou

Gone Are the Days. Thank God.

Sometime in the 80's, I wrote a term paper entitled "Nursing Homes. Warehouses for Death". I had no idea it would get the reaction it got. I was concerned about handing it in to one of our program's most intimidating professors. Having chronicled some of the worst of what I had seen in the care of the elderly, and especially the elderly living with mental illness, I waited for what I thought would be a C+ at best. It was not the type of report that most health care leaders wanted to hear. Not only was it received with an A, it changed my perception of that professor. The experience taught me that sometimes, you just have to *say the words*.

Advances in long-term care in the past 25 years are nothing short of spectacular. Yes, there are still problems. Yes, there are still long waiting lists in many areas. And yes, we as a society have to grapple with the tsunami of baby boomers soon to be requiring 24/7 support or nursing care. However, gone are the days, in the developed world, at least, where 20 or 30 elderly people were housed during the day, in a large common room on mattresses on the floor, wearing diapers and hospital gowns. I saw this on a unit for the elderly, living with what was then considered incurable mental illness. I was there as a nursing student many years ago. Appalled, my colleagues and I reacted by crusading for positive change, some of us becoming professors hoping to inspire students to join us. We crusaded for individual patients and system wide improvements in health care throughout our careers, hoping to make a difference, as corny as it sounds.

Today the care of the elderly, the physically challenged, and those living with all manner of health conditions needing ongoing care is improving greatly. At the same time, we need to prepare ourselves for the caregiver role, to support others who are there, and as a society, improve existing healthcare systems to prepare for difficult times ahead. When the caregiver experiences burnout, not only is she or he in trouble, so is the recipient of care, the family and the community itself. It may take a village to raise a child, and we must now acknowledge it takes a "different thinking" society to care for the frail, the sick, and the elderly in massive numbers.

The Ultimate Burnout

A caregiver is someone whose life is in some way restricted by the need to
be responsible for the care of someone who is mentally ill or handicapped,
physically disabled or whose health is impaired by sickness or old age.

Baroness Pitkeathley[118]

The Baroness' definition of the caregiver, though not the most positive
terminology, is widely accepted for the truth at its core. One can just feel
the burnout approaching, and ask anyone who has been at it for some time;
there is no burn out like caregiver fatigue.

Most caregivers accept their new role with a sense of hope things will go
well. This is good, and the more this type of feeling can be maintained, or
reignited, the better things will go for all involved. There may be a feeling of
idealism, and an eagerness for things to go better than "what we heard".

Typically, at some point, frustration and exhaustion set in. Coupled with
guilt and often less than perfect family dynamics, the caregiver can begin to
feel overwhelmed, like a failure or even... like the family martyr. Without
help, support, reward or least acknowledgment, and a good measure of mental
resiliency, an inability to cope and even illness, are inevitable.

For the purposes of this discussion, the caregiver is the person who is
the main provider of healthcare, and day-to-day support for one or more
dependent persons. In this instance, 'caregiver' is not meant to indicate
standard parental care, though some of the elements can be quite similar, and
for the single parent with little or no support, burnout can be an issue. For the
parents of a child in trouble with drugs, promiscuity or gangs, burnout is of
serious concern, and should be addressed in much the same manner.

Increasingly, the care of the elderly is becoming part of the family's
routine. We are an aging population, and for the most part, the health care
system is poorly prepared to support the massive increase in care requirements
emerging in tandem with our demographic reality. Most of us prefer to live

in our own homes or in some sort of independent living facility for our entire lives. The reality is that at some point, many of us require care, be it a small amount of assistance, or full-blown 24/7 nursing care.

A few Statistics

Data for the US, Canada, Africa and Japan, as with many countries world-wide, indicates caregiver burnout is looming as one of the most critical issues of our society:

- In the United States, 52 million informal and family caregivers provide care to someone aged 20+ who is ill or disabled.[119]
- In 2002, 23% of Canadians aged 45–64 provided care to seniors. Of this group, 70% were also employed. 27% of those aged 45–64 with children at home also cared for seniors. [120]
- In Africa: According to a 2006 study done by USAID, HIV/AIDS is having a devastating effect on households. It has orphaned more children in Africa than in any other part of the world. Studies show that up to 60% of orphaned children, including those orphaned by AIDS, live in grandparent-headed households[121]
- In Japan (Population: 127 million), in 2005, 17% of the population was 65+. By 2020, it is expected 26% of the population will be 65+. Only 22.7% of caregivers are male. About 1/2 of the elderly live with their children, the highest rate for industrialized nations.[122]

It Won't Happen to Me

If you are not already in caregiver situation, have you seriously thought about what your chances are, over your lifespan, of becoming either a caregiver or the recipient of care? Why wait? We plan our careers from the time we are in high school. We plan our weddings, and most of us plan how many children we will have. We plan vacations, and we plan for our retirement. We plan for the care of our animals and plants. How many of us are making decisions, or even starting to think about what types of experiences we plan to have as we approach old age, or should we become responsible for the care of a loved one? And no, we are not the first generation to grapple with this issue. From the 1953 Agnes Rogers article, Harper's Magazine, November 1952:

"A final word to younger women... remember that someday you may be the one of whom a daughter says, 'My mother lives with us.'[123]

Worldwide, finding solutions to the daunting challenge of caring for increasing numbers of those in need worldwide, requires the efforts of government agencies as well as NGOs (non-governmental organizations), the private sector, and individuals (that's us). There are many organizations applying their attention, energy and focus to help us all change the way we think about these issues and look for solutions. They will succeed... and they need volunteers, board members and resources. When you are looking for a place to give a helping hand, even the smallest assistance will be warmly welcomed. For the purposes of this chapter, we will mostly focus on issues faced by individuals, as opposed to society as a whole.

He's in a Nursing Home. Am I Still a Caregiver?

Even when the person requiring care is living in a supportive housing environment or nursing home, the person who is the main support to that individual can still experience caregiver burnout. That person may be very involved with care, decision-making, advocating, shopping, doing laundry, taking their loved one to health care appointments and other outings, and acting as a go-between for the individual in the facility and the rest of the family and friends. This typically involves frequent visits, which require planning, the use of transportation, financial resources and most of all... *time.*

From the outside, to those not so closely involved, it may seem like the visiting caregiver has no potential for burnout. Though this potential is certainly decreased when the care recipient is living in some type of supportive or residential environment, it is there none the less, especially if there is only one person playing this role.

Welcome to the Bubble

I come from a large extended family. I have 79 first cousins for a grand total of all family members weighing in at somewhere around the 250 mark. Large families were common in my parent's generation, and so being one of the few healthcare professionals in the crew, I have frequently been involved in the care circle of relatives from all ends of the spectrum. One day, as my brother, sister-in-law and I were at the deathbed of our beloved, all alone in the world, bachelor Uncle Léo, we came to a conclusion about the syndrome we are experiencing and gave it a name. Whenever we found ourselves involved in one of these care circles, we called it, "being in The Bubble".

Does this sound familiar? While everybody else in the world, it seems, is going about their business, shopping for new clothes, planning a vacation, working on their investments… there *you* are, in a routine that involves spending hours, sometimes days, sometimes overnight stays, at the hospital or nursing home. It involves waiting to ask overworked physicians and nurses pressing questions that they hear on a daily basis, but for you are of utmost importance. Being in the bubble involves being detached somewhat from your normal existence, in order to play the caregiver role for someone you love.

Sometimes being in the bubble involves those last few days of planning a funeral, choosing burial clothing, and hanging out at the funeral home. Take heart, for those of you who haven't been in the bubble yet, there can be enjoyment, there is deep satisfaction, and sometimes there are even a few laughs along the way.

What's the Big Deal? She Loves Him, Doesn't She?

Caregiver burnout is major stress. It presents a danger to both the caregiver and the loved one. It affects attitude, mood and motivation and will eventually affect your health if left unchecked. Occasionally, for those who have not been part of this life scenario, there may be temptation to be somewhat judgmental about the situation, as we look at it from the outside. It is very easy to think, "Well, she's his wife. She's *supposed* to take care of him. She loves him, so for her, it really isn't that stressful."

However, love does not negate the fact that there is a major risk factor at play here, for all manner of conditions such as cardiovascular illness, and especially heart attack and stroke. It is stress. Ongoing, 24/7, high-level, easily ignored stress.

Keep in mind that the caregiver may still be holding down a job, have other family members to take care of, and be experiencing financial difficulties. It is also possible, especially if the person is a new caregiver, that he or she will not really have understood all the responsibilities they have now taken on.

It is much better to understand caregiver burnout and compassion fatigue, to prevent it and deal with it, than to find yourself also in need of health care. **Caregivers, here are a few habits that, left unchecked, *are guaranteed to contribute to you burning out*:**

- Sacrificing your needs on an ongoing basis in order to benefit the other
- Constant agreeing to fulfill the wishes of the other. ("Can't say No" syndrome)
- Difficulty requesting help
- Feeling responsible, or as if you are the only person who can provide the care. ("Only I can do it." syndrome)
- Expectations of yourself are unrealistically high
- Expectations of others are unrealistically high

- A prevailing wish to make things ideal for the care recipient. ("She's so dedicated!" syndrome)

Does any of this sound familiar?

Signs of Caregiver Burnout

If the answer to the above question was "yes", ask yourself if you are experiencing any of the following:

- A feeling of overwhelm, or an increasing inability to get and stay organized
- Easily frustrated, irritable snapping at people you love
- Feelings and outbursts of anger
- Growing or recurring feelings of sadness, loneliness, discouragement and even depression
- Diminishing self-esteem, feelings of worthlessness
- Sleep disturbances
- Frequent colds, or a cold that lasts longer than usual
- Fatigue, quickly exhausted
- Weight fluctuations
- Headaches
- Backaches
- Withdrawing from family and friends
- Difficulty concentrating

Avoid Caregiver Burnout

What is the point of being Superman or Superwoman, if you yourself crumble and fall to insurmountable stress? Isn't it better to limit the demands on yourself, and be able to remain in a more realistic, effective caregiver role for a longer period of time? For countless people living with illnesses and conditions such as stroke, head injury, serious mental illness, multiple sclerosis, and every form of debilitating illness you can think of, sadly, the caregiver is no longer at the bedside. As the months and years go by, without increasing support, the caregiver and family cannot continue and cannot cope, or the caregiver succumbs to their own health crisis. It does not have to be this way.

The Basics

1. Think about your nutrition, sleep and exercise habits, and review them with a health care professional if possible. Begin creating healthier day-to-day lifestyle patterns. Remember, it can take 30 days or more to adopt a new habit.

2. Schedule time for yourself daily, including private time. Schedule breaks at least every two to four weeks, which involve a full 24 to 48 hour period of relaxation. Plan activities or travel you wish to do, without the person requiring care coming along. To do so will probably require you taking advantage of your area's Respite Care, where an agency will take in your loved one overnight and for longer periods, giving you relief. They may have someone come in to your home to provide the Respite Care. Contact your local community healthcare agency to begin inquiries about these resources.

3. Seek out, request, and accept help. Let go of feelings of guilt and begin building a stronger support system. If your care recipient or loved one is mentally competent, begin an open dialogue, where you feel free to define your own limitations, and to talk about what you are prepared to do. Talk about what you are able to do, and what you may not be able to do, on an ongoing basis. Help them understand that as the care requirements increase, you will not be able to manage it all on your own. If you require help to facilitate these discussions, there may be a family member, friend or member of the healthcare

team such as a social worker, who would be more than ready and able to join you in the discussion, or to help prepare you to open the conversation with your loved one. There may be adult day care centers, and even in-home respite care available in your area.

4. If you are not already using the Internet, looking for solutions to your care giving issues, now is the time to start. A mountain of resources is there to help you, with ideas for all aspects of care giving. Choose a legitimate source from your area or country.

5. Join your local caregiver support group. Many other people are going through the same things you are, right now, or they have 'been there'. It is amazing how much strength you will gain, from speaking with others. You may even learn tips and hear about ideas that you had not thought of. You may find out about resources you were unaware of. *If there is no such group in your area, start one.* Put up some flyers, an ad in a newspaper or on your free TV community news Channel. Hold a first coffee meeting in your living room. Don't worry, build it and they will come.

Healthier Thinking for the Caregiver

1. Do your planning in small increments: one week at a time, or even one day at a time, may be all you can do for now.

2. Remember that your reality is greatly driven by what is going on between your ears. Any strategy that helps you change your thoughts from negative upsetting ones, to more positive, supportive, hopeful ones, can dramatically change your situation and your actual experience.

3. Learn to let go of negative feelings such as resentment and guilt. There are many techniques for this, and like anything else, practice makes perfect. Go back to the first section of this book for ideas. For many caregivers, just the thought of letting go of their feelings of

total dedication is unfathomable. However, as with any other skill, this healthy thinking strategy can be learned, and be one of your greatest allies.

4. Re-acquaint yourself with your sense of humor. Tap into it, develop it, and use whatever works to get you laughing at least once a day, preferably three times a day. Look for comedies on television. Start a collection of funny movies, look up public domain movies to watch free of charge online, or search for your favorite funny topics on YouTube. Do whatever it takes to get into the habit of having a good belly laugh as often as possible. If you are going to the movies, make sure it is uplifting, or a comedy that will send you home swimming in endorphins (a hormone that makes you feel good, relieves stress, decreases pain…). Seek out a laughter therapy group in your area, and join in this therapeutic fun.

5. Develop new interests. You have never had a hobby? Now is the time to pick up the guitar, a paintbrush, get some power tools. You will be surprised at how energizing it is to start being creative again. By focusing on learning to paint, do woodwork, sing in the choir or any other thing you have always wanted to do. There is always a way for you to carve out time at least once a week to start a new, enjoyable activity.

6. If you are "in for the long haul" caregiver role, if you are committed to hanging in there, deepen your ability to practice patience. *Letting go* strategies will help tremendously with this. Anger, mistrust and outbursts of frustration will backfire on you and increase your stress level, making you a walking time bomb. When you find yourself losing your patience, step back, physically remove yourself if you can, and apply your attention to thinking of some creative solutions to the problem at hand. Call a support person or support group for the condition your loved one is living with. For example, there are

support groups for Alzheimer's in most areas, with many of them having contact persons for you to speak with today.

7. Practice a "wait and see" approach for what can, and cannot be done.

8. Be ready for anything. Develop a flexible approach to your expectations and decisions.

9. Have some healthy satisfying sex.

10. Think of your loved one as the same person he or she always was, with the disease process or condition giving them different characteristics. Avoid thinking of them as your "patient."

At the end of this chapter is an easy meditation, especially for caregivers. Try it tonight, as you are drifting off to sleep.

A Caring Question

I cannot leave this chapter without this one most important element for everyone who knows a caregiver. Do not kid yourself; even if this person does not speak of it, he or she is experiencing challenges. The best thing you can say to your caregiver friend or neighbour is not, "Let me know if you need anything." It is rather,

> **"What can I do to help?** *I have an hour right now.*"

Or maybe you have an afternoon next week. Be specific and offer specific help. The statement, "let me know if you need anything" puts most people in the uncomfortable situation of having to ask. The second question, "What can I do to help?" is dramatically different. It is you rolling up your sleeves, jumping in and doing something. You might also want to think about offering this help not only to the caregiver individual, but also to the family as a whole.

Just you being able to give them respite, for one overnight break, or even one hour can make all the difference for that person and that family.

Regardless of whether or not you play the caregiver role in your own old age, why not take every healthy thinking strategy, and every decision possible to make it a success story? The following page is a meditation exercise for caregivers. It is easily adapted to any situation.

"We have to start changing the way we think about family caregivers. The real solution lies in a wholesale change in perspective."
Neena Chappell, Gerontologist[124]

Notes:

Meditation for the Caregiver

Decide that you will do this meditation exercise tonight as you are drifting off to sleep. Make sure that your bed is as comfortable as you can make it. If you have not gotten around to doing it for a while, this might be the time to put on some fresh sheets before you call it a night.

1. Take a warm shower or bath, and wear your most comfortable sleepwear for the night.

2. Complete all your usual bedtime routines, ensuring you will not have to get up again.

3. Go to bed. Make yourself as comfortable as possible, and take three effective breaths. Use the following 4-7-8 breathing pattern[125] as an example:

   A. Breathe in through your nose for 4 seconds, deep enough that your belly rises as you do so.
   B. Hold the breath for up to 7 seconds if you can.
   C. Breathe out, slowly, through your mouth, for 8 seconds if possible.
   D. Repeat 3 times.

Now begin creating the following mental scenario, eyes closed and breathing comfortably.

In your mind, go to your favorite relaxing outdoor setting. It could be a beautiful garden, a mountain, the beach, or a meadow. The choice is yours. Picture it in the most beautiful way possible. Try to imagine the actual colors and everything you would like to see hear and smell around you.

Continue breathing comfortably, relaxed.

Imagine that everyone you love is being taken care of by someone else. The people caring for your loved ones are highly skilled, gentle people who have a special relationship with all the people receiving their attention. Imagine that everything your loved one needs is automatically taken care of in the best way possible. All your normal responsibilities are taken care of by the care team.

Imagine that there is a beautiful enclosure, gate or fence all around your area. This fence is beautiful, with a gate for you to go through at any time you wish. On the other side of the gate is a group of helpful, caring people, whose only purpose in life, is to assist you with every possible need and desire you have. Imagine that you spend as long as you wish in your special place, enjoying whatever activity you wish. Imagine yourself reading, watching a wonderful movie on a television, playing just for you, while you sit in the most comfortable lounging chair you have ever been in. Or perhaps you are enjoying your special time by working on your classic car, polishing it and getting it ready to take a ride down the coastal highway.

Create whatever scenario you wish tonight as you drift off to sleep and continue thinking through your scenario until you do so. If you begin to feel restless at any time, repeat the breathing exercise. Continue to enjoy your visual experience until you drift off to sleep.

Enjoy!

Chapter 7

Health & Wellness

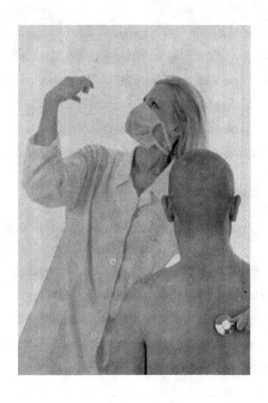

Not exercising is like taking a depressant.

Dr. Tal Ben Sharar[125]

Use It or Lose It

This chapter is for those times when we fall off the health wagon. It is also for the person who has been trying to ignore the barrage of 'how to get/stay healthy' information that we are bombarded with. You may have picked up this book because you had a wake-up call about your own health. Highly possible, because, being human, we are remarkably skilled at ignoring what we know we should be doing, and instead, going about our lives mostly doing what feels good at the time. Instead, let's try something different.

In Case You Stop Here

In case you stop reading here, as a minimum, please do this:

- Improve and multiply your Family and Friends circle. Take care of those relationships, and focus on the ones that feel the best.
- Do less, not more. Get present. That means stop doing 14 things at once. Turn of your BB in meetings, and at home. Focus on whatever you are doing, and *only* that. Take breaks every 2-3 hours, a real lunch, a good sleep nightly and a vacation week every 3-4 months.
- Simplify everything. Do you need to hand out a 30-page document, or can the salient points fit on a One-Pager?
- Get moving. Immobility leads to nasty health problems in all areas of your mind and body, including cardiac death and depression. 30 minutes a day. Start now.

- Wear a helmet if you are doing anything that may cause your head to suddenly come into contact with another object.
- Get a complete health assessment from a nurse practitioner or a physician.

A Model for Wellness

On the next page is my **HELP ! Wellness Model**, a conceptual image to help you stay focused when you face a real health *problem*.

Note: First, I am avoiding using the trendy word "challenge" right now. No patient or client I have ever worked with has ever said to me, "Gisèle, I have a health challenge. Can you help?" No. They say, "Gisèle, can you help me, I've got a health problem." Secondly, as you have probably noticed, I also avoid the word "client", when speaking of people who need health care. Though the term has far-reaching use in academia, and in some health care documentation, any person I have ever taken care of wants to be referred to as "patient", not client. So, for my friends and colleagues in academia, bear with me.

A model is a way of looking at issues, ideas and possible solutions. The types of models most effective in triggering positive, sustainable change are those, which are visual, and super-simple. Have you noticed that when you are really stressed… when you are in big trouble, the more complicated your instructions are, the less you can grasp their meaning, and actually put it into practice? Have you ever received one of those booklets from a well-meaning person, from which you are supposed to start a new health program, and it is about 70 pages long… and you need a medical dictionary to use it?

The HELP ! Wellness Model is a simple visual representation of *what works*, when we are faced with the diagnosis of illness, an injury or any other health problem/issue/condition.

HELP ! Wellness Model ©

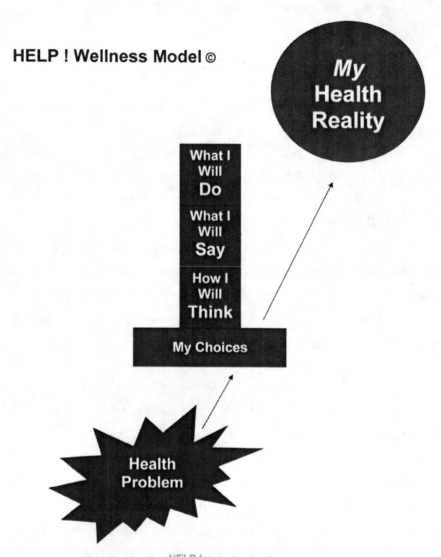

You have been diagnosed with a health condition, or you have had an injury, or you are living with a health problem. You have a desire to make the absolute best of it, and join the ranks of those who do really well with this diagnosis.

You might be discouraged right now, but you will be amazed at how much better you will do, by applying these ideas. If you are conscious and still able to read or hear, you can, or you with the help of others, can move forward with making your situation the absolute best that it can be.

The first thing I want you to do is look at the model on the previous page, and start at the bottom of the page, where you see an "explosion-like" image, containing the words *Health Problem*.

What is Your Problem?

Begin by knowing and accepting what your condition really is. Go back and review the "Accept" strategies in Section 1 if you need to.

Do you really understand what your primary health care provider has told you? Stressed by the initial shock of receiving a diagnosis, we often misunderstand what we have just been told. This happens to everybody. It has happened to me. Be courageous. Leave shyness, embarrassment and fear of looking stupid at home. This is your life. Ask for explanation, and for the information to be repeated as often as you need it. Ask questions. From there, collect the information you need to educate yourself about your condition. Your health care provider can give you some current written information about your health problem, or tell you where to get it. Your community health organizations, public health agencies and social service groups are a source of information as well the self-help organizations for your particular condition (E.g.: heart, stroke[126], cancer[127]).

Hint: You know you're on the healthy thinking track, because though it may be frightening at first, just knowing more about what you have will *feel* better... knowledge is power.

Choices. Choices. Choices.

We make choices based on our ego, our intelligence and cognitive ability, on our level of need to be liked, accepted and respected. We make choices based on our level of education, formal or informal, on the choices our loved ones make, and sometimes out of desperation. So what now?

Now that you understand and have accepted your health problem, you need to start making choices. Now, along with your research about the condition itself, you will have collected some information, advice and recommendations about how to manage it, cure it or heal it. If you are facing a chronic disease* such as asthma, diabetes, heart disease, or AIDS, you should now 'rev up' your use of healthy thinking > speaking > action. Choosing to wallow in the negative facts about your condition feels really bad, doesn't it? That habit can actually contribute to you becoming depressed, on top of this condition. Depression itself is one of the world's leading causes of disability, and if that is what you are facing already, these strategies will help, and you probably need the support and partnership of a licensed health care professional to help you get through the toughest parts.

*For applying your energy, attention and focus to *not* getting a chronic disease, the next web site you visit should be one of these:

- Center for Disease Control and Prevention (US) http://www.cdc. gov/pcd/
- World Health Organization Chronic Disease Prevention Fact Sheets http://www.who.int/dietphysicalactivity/publications/facts/en/
- Dr. Roizen's RealAge interactive fun web site http://www.realage. com/. Having fun with our health strategies is a golden key to succeeding ☺ .Corny, but true.

Choice # 1. How I Will *Think*

Inner Dialogue.

When a child is having trouble with something, do we say,

"Yes, you're right. It's too hard. Riding a bicycle is not for you, sweetie…"

I hope not. Our natural instinct is to encourage the child, and come up with something realistically optimistic, like,

"I fell off a lot when I was learning too. It hurt a bit, but I got back on, and look at me now!"

What type of messaging are you giving yourself in your thinking choices concerning your health problem? Are you developing resilience or defeat? Whether or not you were an optimist before this, now is the time to get good at it. You will also find, due to the contagious nature of optimism, that even your health care providers will be, well… *more* helpful! It is automatic: even the most professional health care providers naturally feel more satisfaction helping those who are actively showing they want to succeed. And what do we do when something satisfies us, when it makes *us* feel good? We want to do it again.

Ignore any Gloomer Doomer telling you that healthy positive thinking is useless. Put your blinders on, and protect your most precious resource… the power between your ears. This is the time to find some effective ways to think about your issue. "A-Statements" (affirmation-type statements that feel real) such as,

- "I think I could do as well as Halle Berry, in my life with diabetes."[128]

- "If Quincy Jones can be well after a massive brain aneurysm, I can too."[130]

Remember: the A-Statement has to make you feel good when you think about it. If one does not work, try something that makes you feel even a tiny bit better.

Let's say, for example, that you have been told that you have infertility, and will not be able to bear a child. Once the initial shock, acute anger and deep sadness wears off, it probably *will not* feel good to try saying to yourself,
"Oh, it's ok, now we can just go on, and look for other aspects of life to focus on."
Though there may be some truth to that thought, and eventually the nugget of truth that may be within it could be of value to you, it probably will not feel good right at this moment. Instead, look for "A-Statements" to think about that are more like this,

- "Well. Now we know. I also know, that eventually, I will not feel this emotional pain as acutely as I do right now. I know I will cry, and yes, I know I will get through this, and look for joy. I know I will find it. For today, I will do one special thing for myself that I usually enjoy, that I have not done for some time."
- "I will look for someone who has been through it. I know it will feel good to talk to someone. We will find ways to overcome our frustration. We love each other, and we will get through this."

Inner Experiences.

Now is the time to adopt positive relaxation habits… for life. Starting today, begin a daily practice of meditating , daydreaming… whatever you want to call it, with a focus on finding *thoughts that feel good to you*. This could be simply,

- thinking about nothing in particular… just resting and relaxing with my eyes closed, counting my breathing
- imagining a coloured screen, and breathing a bit more regularly and deeper than I was before I began the relaxation
- sitting with eyes closed, letting the mind wander and replacing negative thoughts with better ones
- a more specific guided meditation[129]
- developing pleasant, healthy mental images, which you can 'pull up' at any time

Note: The American Journal of Cardiology has published several studies promoting meditation, including one 18-year study showing that seniors who meditated daily lived an average of 23% longer that normal for their age group.[130]

Daydream

Don't knock it. Scientists (Einstein was a great daydreamer), experts from the field of psychology, psychiatry, nursing, medicine and other health professionals are telling us to use this powerful tool at our disposal, due to its beneficial effect on our health. Kalina Christoff, a professor at UBC Department of Psychology reports from a recent study, that scientific findings suggest,

"Daydreaming, which can occupy as much as one third of our waking lives, is an important cognitive state where we may unconsciously turn our attention from immediate tasks to sort through important problems in our lives."[131]

How you choose to think, as you begin to manage or live with this, is your decision. You can think like Einstein, and end up solving problems by daydreaming. Or you can hang on to the "worst case scenario" file of thoughts that can easily occupy your mind when you are living with illness.

Choose some encouraging scenarios to daydream about, related to your health, and start today… maybe right now. My grandmother Zelda was a daydreamer. She lived with diabetes… to the age of 99.

Note to Professionals: One word. Burnout. Is your work stressful? Are you generally overworked or overwhelmed? How will you fare, if on top of that you are diagnosed with a chronic illness, or suffer an injury? Or, perhaps you are already in that boat. Get a grip on just how much you can handle, and make some life saving decisions now if you need to think differently. Dr. Brian Goldman's article on physician burnout says it all.[132] The provocative, "tell it like it is" Canadian physician offers a wake up call,

"But everyone has limits. The trick is to know and live according to them."

How can you change your thinking, now?

Choice #2. What I Will *Say*

What story will you tell? This is where you make choices about your words. You will choose the conversations you will have, and the story you will tell yourself and others. Especially about your health issue. By now, you understand that thinking negatively is counterproductive to healing. Let's take it a step further.

You are visiting your aunt Charita and your uncle Aadi. Unfortunately, they have the flu: they have contracted H1N1… the swine flu virus. Managing fairly well, they have typical flu symptoms… aches and pains, fever, loss of appetite, cough, and they feel pretty lousy. Charita is taking it all in stride, following the nurse's advice, and resting much of the time. Her mood is optimistic, and she is accepting the illness, and looking forward to feeling better. This is the story she is telling.

Aadi, on the other hand, is upset at the whole scenario, angry at "whoever gave him this disease!" not drinking the fluids recommended, because it is painful to swallow, and he is constantly complaining about being stuck in the house. This is the story he is telling.

As the days go by, Charita gets better, and is puttering in the garden two weeks later, while Aadi is now complaining she is pulling the weeds out incorrectly... as he coughs and shivers with yet another bout of fever.

This example is obviously an exaggeration; however, it is important for you to understand the negative effect of complaining, on your overall health status. I dare say that excessive complaining could actually slow your recovery. If there is one thing science is quite sure about at this point, is that the very thing that responds the best to your own thoughts is your own body. In fact, if it were up to Dr. Phil[133], he would observe the complaining and say to Aadi, "How's *that* workin' for you?"

Choose a Better Story.

Instead of complaining, do state the facts about any signs and symptoms for which you are seeking diagnosis, treatment or relief, when in assessment conversation with your health care professionals. Do tell your loved ones of any major issues, and particular problems, especially when they are inquiring, and when they are there to help you with your health needs. However, once that conversation is over, and relief has been sought and gained when possible, or you have made a decision to take action if things really are not going well... change your story.

Catch yourself in repetitive story telling about your condition, tests you had, treatments you are hoping for, the good or bad care you received, and any information about your condition. If you are not catching yourself in repetitive plaintiff style story telling... believe me, your friends and family are. You may even begin to notice certain people distancing themselves from you. If this is happening, in all probability, they still love you… they are just bored to tears with The Story. It can happen to anyone.

"So what *do* I talk about?" you ask. So many things… so many choices… the latest good news you found out about, a book you are reading, a CD you got, an activity you would like to take up, someone you heard from recently, a million things… just get some new stories. In fact, if you can give as much attention, energy and focus to the idea of wellness, as you have been giving to the fact of your health problem… you may surprise yourself with the progress you will make. You may in fact, attract a lot less of what you do not want, and a lot more of what you do want.

Find something to be passionate about. Rose, my friend from the Death & Dying chapter, was passionate about communicating, having fun, learning and looking good, to the end. She had a stash of fine wine in her room to celebrate with friends when they visited, she was always reading something, and… she enjoyed putting on her makeup* every day. That was her story. People loved visiting her, and the biggest problem on the palliative care unit for the nurses caring for her, was crowd control.

Choose a better story.

Note: Look Good Feel Better[134] is a support program for people living with cancer, now operating in many countries. Look for it in your area.

Choice # 3. What I Will *Do*

Let's assume now that you have accepted your health problem. If you have not, you will not be able to take appropriate action. The battle between your desire for a miracle and your need to follow the best health advice known to the human race is a risky one. I am not saying there is no such thing as a miracle… I have experienced or been a witness to a few events amazing enough that people are still shaking their heads

However, the person who is living with one leg due to an amputation at this time in the chronology of medical discovery (we're in 2010) is not able to grow another leg (although I did see someone who experienced the re-growth of a finger tip by using "Pixie Dust" bio-engineered from a pig's bladder lining cells. The video link is in the endnotes[135].).

What that person *can* do, however, is think of, tell a story of, and *act towards* getting the most amazing prosthesis… maybe one day, one that is exactly like the other leg… one that moves, feels, and has hair! Medical miracles are being developed, and with the collaboration of technology and medicine, the future is hopeful.

And so, your **"What I Will Do"** work is to **seek out, and begin following, the most highly recommended health practices known, pertaining to your condition.**

And while you're at it, learn how to prevent other health conditions from becoming part of your reality. Just because you have "Diagnosis A" does not mean you are done now, you have been dealt your hand, and are no longer at risk for "Diagnosis B, C and D". If your problem is lung cancer, for example, and you know that generally, walking 30 minutes a day is now recommended for overall health and prevention of heart disease, and if that is not possible for you right now, what type of exercise *is* possible? Can you do Range Of Motion exercises? How about isometric exercises? Have you asked to see a physiotherapist to get you on the right track? Talk to your primary health care provider, and work on a health plan that will put *you* in the best possible position to do well. Become an expert on your condition.

Your Health Reality

Determined, healthy thinking people do amazing things… even when they have major health problems. They are following a plan that looks something like our "HELP ! Wellness Model." You have much more control over your health destiny than you think, especially if right now you are still in the early stages of a serious diagnosis, or just had a serious injury. You cannot expect your thinking process to be as healthy right now, as it could be over the next few months, if you make the decision to take charge of your future. Do not take my word for it; seek out these people's stories:

- <u>Lance Armstrong</u>. Was diagnosed with advanced cancer of the testicles, which had metastasized to his lungs and brain. That was 1996. We are in 2010. He is still riding his bike professionally and founded LiveStrong, to help fight Cancer. [136]

- <u>Patty Duke</u>. Was not diagnosed until she was in her 30's, she suffered with Bipolar Disorder and is now an advocate for mental health, and a still a successful actor. [137]

- <u>Davina Marcia Herbert Ingrams, 18th Baroness Darcy de Knayth</u>. Her husband was killed in a car crash that left her paralyzed from the neck down, in 1964. She regained some movement in her upper body, became a politician (House of Lords), promoted the interest of children with special needs, and helped launch the Paralympic games. She died in 2008.[138]

- <u>Annette Funicello</u>. First noticing symptoms of MS (Multiple Sclerosis) in 1987, Annette continued to work in movies for some time, and retired to become an advocate for the fight against MS. In 2002, Annette accepted the role of Ambassador for the Society's Walk MS event. [139]

Prevention

What if you could live your entire life, never needing a 24/7 caregiver, and never needing to live anywhere other than in your own home? Millions of elderly are experiencing exactly that. These are the people who have been successful in their planning, decision making and have taken the road less travelled… the healthier road. For those of us serious about living long and healthy independent lives well into our 90s, and even past 100, there is no getting around it; the following basic healthy living patterns are required:

- Healthy nutritional habits, such as a daily food intake which is low in salt, sugar, fat and alcohol, high in fibre, and which contains the recommended daily allowances of all vitamins and minerals as per the most current research.
- 30 minutes a day of walking or similar exercise
- A positive, optimistic outlook on life which includes openness to new ideas and the development and maintenance of healthy relationships
- The understanding and adopting of habits such as the **prevention** of falls, infectious disease, environmental and workplace related illness and other conditions which could threaten our independence and life

The above habits are not "you"? Are you serious about living old and healthy? You might want to think again. While we're at it, let's look at the thinking habits of the oldest healthiest people in all countries.

Being Positive May Add 7.5 Years to Your Life

How do you look at getting older? It is possible that your perception of aging will affect your lifespan. The Ohio Longitudinal Study of Aging and Retirement findings: even after accounting for factors such as, gender, age, loneliness, financial status and health, people with *more positive perceptions of their own aging* lived approximately 7.5 years longer than others did. The study included over 600 people, for a period of 23 years.[140] As yet, researchers have not been able to figure out "Why would a positive attitude lead to a longer life?" Can healthy thinking about aging improve our will to live? Can it make us more resistant to illness? Would we be more proactive about our own health? The Ohio group thinks it may be possible that the mental stress of aging is lessened in people who have a positive attitude. Why not develop the attitude of looking forward to aging, *before* you get there?

What is so Great About Aging?

Most of our societies value youth and beauty above age and wisdom. The less than pleasant aspects about aging are more frequently emphasized in the media. However, maturity and being able to draw from a wide variety of experiences actually gives us more insight as we get older, and the ability to make better and better decisions as time goes on. All else positive about aging stems from there. Though the possibility of experiencing these features of aging depends on many factors, here are a few:

- The ability to choose our day-to-day activities
- Having more time to do creative work
- Increased possibilities for leisure activity
- For most people, having developed a circle of family and friends to enjoy
- For those who decide to make it a priority, increased possibility of health and wellness well into old age.
- A more mellow, wiser perspective is usually experienced, with resulting respect increasing by other generations
- Confidence and a strong sense of self are typical.
- Motivation is usually high, including a thirst for knowledge and experiences. As the clock ticks… there is no time to waste.
- Pleasure from a life well-lived

Longevity Boosters

Aside from learning new skills to maximize your brainpower as you age, there are standard factors, which have been studied repeatedly, and are now understood to add significantly to our lifespan. The following five are the most widely studied and reported, with various studies revealing some differences in the number of years added.

1. Healthy weight: up to 3 years longer

2. Exercising regularly: up to 3 years longer

3. Normal blood pressure levels: up to 4 years longer

4. Normal cholesterol levels: up to 4 years longer

5. Not smoking: up to 14 years longer

One of the most useful and reliable sources for information about staying healthy is your area's public health organization. These are all easily found on the internet, or in your phone book. The information available through these organizations is evidence-based, current, and seeks to offer advice in line with highly respected sources such as the World Health Organization.

You have an inner strength you may not have known existed.
You have the strength to choose.

To live the best possible reality for your health problem, you must
choose the way you think,
what you say and
what you do.

Notes

Conclusion

The Lion Within

You have power within that will sustain you through the most terrifying experiences. Through adversity, we grow closer to those who love us and support us. Even people from "dysfunctional families" can succeed in times of trouble, and when it is the best option, perhaps build new, healthier families and networks of real friends.

Perhaps it is time to start building your Tribe. Strengthen old and new relationships. Spend more and more of your time with people you feel *in sync* with. Spend less time with who people who leave you feeling exhausted, frustrated and who contribute in some way to lowering your self-esteem. Do we not find out who our true friends are in times of trouble? I have had friends show up in the bubble, at the most amazing times, to lend a hand, sometimes friends I had not seen in years. Your Tribe can be your greatest ally.

You have an opportunity to re-invent your self, every day, and when life throws you a curve, what do you have to lose? Explore. Create. Open your mind to your own talents, that otherwise may have been left on the shelf.

Simplify your life by changing the way you think.

Think it. See it. Say it and Do it.

Slow down. Focus on the things that are important to you… the people, activities, experiences that make you *feel* good, and *are* good for you.

The spirit of the Lion is within you. It is a healthy spirit, a good spirit, nourished by your thoughts. It is a spirit and a power that no one can ever take away from you. It will serve you well, all your days.

About the Author

With over 30 years of health care service, from the bedside to the corner office, Gisèle Guénard is an award winning leader in the positive change movement, an author and sought after keynote speaker. Her problem solving philosophy is based on Einstein's, "We can only solve a problem by changing the thinking that created it."

HELP! Healthy Thinking in Times of Trouble is the partner book to her her first in the series, Attract It. *Beyond* Positive Thinking. "I had to write HELP!," Gisèle says, "to help people with the dilemma… 'I am thinking positive,but what do I do when something bad happens?'"

In 2007, Gisèle founded VisionarEase Inc., specializing in Positive Change Leadership & Consulting. Thousands have been inspired by her message to move through adversity, and to reach for what they truly want in life.

No stranger to tragedy, including the death of beloved friends and close family, she shares a deep connection with those who face major struggles.

Gisèle believes that we have a responsibility to share our success strategies, and use our skills and influence to literally save our planet, heal our civilization and *change the world*.

Fluent in French and in English, Gisèle holds a Bachelor of Science (Nursing) degree from Laurentian University, as well as a Master of Education degree from the University of Toronto.

Gisèle and her husband John live in Ontario, Canada, enjoying a life filled with family, friends, music, nature and joy.

Visit Gisèle at the VisionarEase website www.visionarease.com .

Endnotes Comments Resources

1   **Preface**

Guénard, Giséle, ATTRACT IT. *BEYOND* POSITIVE THINKING, (iUniverse, Bloomington, IN, 2008, 2nd Edition), http://www.amazon. ca/Attract-Positive-Thinking-Gisele-Guenard/dp/0595433774

Introduction

2   Magical thinking is just that. Any unfounded, hocus-pocus type of thinking that "just wishing will make it so", or "a magic genie will give me what I want", or "all I need is a visual image of it, and it will come", or "new age thinking 'X' will bring me the lottery". This type of thinking is unhealthy, and can be a risk factor to anyone living with mental illness.

3   WILLINGNESS TO HELP, Journal of Personality and Social Psychology, 2009, content.apa.org/journals/psp/52/4/721.html

SECTION 1. 10 Strategies for Healthy Thinking

4   Murray, William Hutchinson, THE SCOTTISH HIMALAYAN EXPEDITIONS (J.M. Dent & Sons, London 1951)

5   Byrne, Rhonda et al, THE SECRET, http://www.thesecret.tv/

6   Mayo Clinic teaching page: POSITIVE THINKING: REDUCE STRESS, ENJOY LIFE MORE. http://www.mayoclinic.com/health/positive-thinking/SR00009

7   Tolle, Eckhart, A NEW EARTH, (Penguin, New York, 2006)

8   Center for Disease Control, SPANISH INFLUENZA 1918 http://
www.cdc.gov/ncidod/EID/vol12no01/05-0979.htm

9   Steiner Rice, Helen, This Too Shall Pass Away. Copyrighted to the Helen
Steiner Rice Foundation.

10   Julli, Cathy, THE POWERLESSNESS OF POSITIVE THINKING,
Maclean online. Researchers: Joanne V. Wood, Psychologist (University
of Waterloo) co-author of the soon-to-be-published research article,
John W. Lee (University of Western Ontario) and W.Q. Elaine
Perunovic (University of New Brunswick). The Macleans article is at
http://www2.macleans.ca/2009/07/06/the-powerlessness-of-positive-
thinking/

11   A-STATEMENT: HEALTHY THINKING STRATEGY http://
www.womens-law-of-attraction-solutions.com/credit-card-debt-relief.
html

12   Goodall, Jane, CBC Radio Interview, YES, WE CAN SAVE THE
PLANET, Sept 25 2009

13   Tindle, Hilary A., et al, OPTIMISM, CYNICAL HOSTILITY, AND
INCIDENT CORONARY HEART DISEASE AND MORTALITY
IN THE WOMEN'S HEALTH INITIATIVE, *Circulation.* 2009,
American Heart Association, Inc. The important study is operating
under the title of WOMEN'S HEALTH INITIATIVE, with
information widely available in the public domain, including sites
for participants of the study.

14   Giltay, Dr. Erik J., et al, ARNHEM ELDERLY STUDY, Archives of
General Psychiatry: November 2004

15   Ibid

16   MacDonald, Shauna, News Canada, BLINDNESS TOP HEALTH
FEAR, re-printed in The Sudbury Star, Sept 19 2009

17   Twersky, Jacob, THERE IS NO DARKNESS, the Reader's Digest,
October 1948, Montréal, Canada

18   Gladwell, Malcolm, BLINK, THE POWER OF THINKING WITHOUT THINKING, (Little, Brown & Co., New York, 2005)

19   Northern Life, POLITICIANS CALL FOR INQUEST INTO CULVERT COLLAPSE, May 23 2006. Teen driver, Skye Whitman of Worthington Ontario was killed after her vehicle hit a section of washed out road after a culvert gave way, in 2006.

20   Blanchard, Normand, on Patricia O'Connell Killen and John de Beer's, THE ART OF THEOLOGICAL REFLECTION, (The Crossroad Publishing Company)

21   Patanjali. THE YOGA SUTRAS OF PATANJALI: A NEW TRANSLATION AND COMMENTARY. Edited by Georg Feuerstein. Folkstoone, UK: Dawson, 1979.

22   Virtue, Dr. Doreen, http://www.angeltherapy.com/

23   Guénard, Gisèle, 2-STEP POSITIVE CHANGE STRATEGY©, WOMEN. CHOOSE YOUR THOUGHTS – CHANGE YOUR LIFE! Workshop, visionarease.com Events

24   Einstein, Albert, Letter of 1950, as quoted in The New York Times (29 March 1972) and The New York Post (28 November 1972)

25   JOYFUL NOISE PLAYLIST, at GoodFilm4u , on YouTube , at http://www.youtube.com/user/goodfilm4u

26   Elizabeth Smart, SIX YEARS LATER, Oprah.com, http://www.oprah.com/slideshow/oprahshow/20080826_tows_smart/2

27   St. Petersburg Times online, TO SAVE HIS LIFE, HIKER CUTS OFF ARM, Tampa Bay, May 3, 2003

28   Dyer, Dr. Wayne W., THE POWER OF INTENTION, (Carlsbad, California Hay House, 2004)

29   TrueCowboy.com ,THE STETSON HAT HISTORY,, http://www.truecowboy.com/stetson.php

30   Steinert online, THE HISTORY OF WORLD WAR II MEDICINE, http://home.att.net/~steinert/

31   TURNING CRISIS INTO OPPORTUNITY ™, is a workshop trademarked by VisionarEase Inc. , http://visionarease.com

32   Flexpaths, Press Release, RECESSION IS NO OBSTACLE FOR NEW COMPANY AND PRODUCT LAUNCH, May 20th 2008

33   Reiner, Dr. Robert H., CREATIVE ACTIVITY BENEFICIAL / BIOFEEDBACK STUDY, Department of Psychiatry, New York University Medical Center, study published at large and in the Journal of the American Medical Association,

34   Mandela, Nelson Rolihlahla, LONG WALK TO FREEDOM, (Back Bay Books, USA, 1994)

35   Sultanoff , Dr. Steven M. LEVITY DEFIES GRAVITY; USING HUMOR IN CRISIS SITUATION, THERAPEUTIC HUMOR, American Association for Therapeutic Humor, Summer, 1995

36   (A) Wellcome Trust, LAUGH AND THE WHOLE WORLD LAUGHS WITH YOU: WHY THE BRAIN JUST CAN'T HELP ITSELF. (Science Daily, 2006, December 13)

(B) University of Maryland School of Medicine , UNIVERSITY OF MARYLAND SCHOOL OF MEDICINE STUDY SHOWS LAUGHTER HELPS BLOOD VESSELS FUNCTION BETTER, (Press release, , March 7th, 2005)   Dr. Michael Miller's research indicates that laughter is linked to healthy functioning of blood vessels. Laughter seems to help the inner lining of blood vessels to dilate, increasing blood flow. This benefit was increased in 19 of 20 volunteers after they viewed movie segments that produced laughter. Overall, average blood flow increased 22 percent during laughter, and decreased 35 percent during mental stress.

37   Aburdene, Patricia, MEGATRENDS 2010, (Hampton Roads Publishing Company Inc., Charlottesville, VA, 2005)

38   Smart, Elizabeth et al (U.S. Department of Justice, Office of Justice Programs, Office of Juvenile Justice and Delinquency Prevention)

YOU'RE NOT ALONE. THE JOURNEY FROM ABDUCTION TO EMPOWERMENT (Washington, DC, 2005) The book is available free as a PDF online at http://www.ncjrs.gov/pdffiles1/ojjdp/221965.pdf

39   The Oprah Show Interview with Elizabeth Smart (September 10, 2008) http://www.oprah.com/slideshow/oprahshow/20080826_tows_smart

40   Freedman, Rich, VALLEJO WOMAN HELPS ENCOURAGE 'END STAGE' CANCER PATIENTS,   Times-Herald, Posted by the Good News Network. www.goodnewsnetwork.org

41   Salbi, Zainab & Beckland, Laurie, BETWEEN TWO WORLDS: ESCAPE FROM TYRRANY: GROWING UP IN THE SHADOW OF SADDAM, (Gotham books, New York, NY 2005). Women for Women International is at http://www.womenforwomen.org .

42   UNFPA, the United Nations Population Fund CALLING FOR AN END TO FEMALE GENITAL MUTILATION/CUTTING, http://www.unfpa.org/gender/practices1.htm

43   Tarrant, David, NORMAN BORLAUG, NOBEL LAUREATE FOR FIGHTING FAMINE, DIES, DAVID TARRANT, The Dallas Morning News, September 13, 2009

44   Contributing sources for the Norman Borlaug story: www.goodnewsnetwork.com, The Daily Morning News, the Associated Press

45   Espanola General Hospital,   ESPANOLA & AREA FAMILY HEALTH TEAM page http://esphosp.on.ca : Also, see Comparison of Canadian Primary Health Care Models , by Julie MacDonald, Research Fellow, The University of New South Wales.

46   Ontario Ministry of Health and Long-Term Care, NURSE PRACTITIONER-LED PRIMARY CARE CLINICS, http://www.

health.gov.on.ca/english/public/updates/archives/hu_03/docnurse/
hu_nurses.html

47   Butcher, Marilyn & Heale, Roberta, Sudbury District Nurse
        Practitioner Clinic, CANADA'S FIRST NURSE PRACTITIONER-
        LED PRIMARY HEALTH CARE CLINIC, http://sdnpc.ca/

48   FREE THE CHILDREN, http://www.freethechildren.com/

49   OPRAH'S ANGEL NETWORK, http://oprahsangelnetwork.org/

50   Gladwell, Malcolm, THE TIPPING POINT, (Back Bay books/Little,
        Brown & Co., New York, NY)

SECTION 2. Help for the Human Journey

Chapter 1. Mental Health Challenges

51   Dr. Oz five strategies are widely publicized. He has recently launched
        his own television program. http://www.doctoroz.com/

52   Caplan, Paula J., THEY SAY YOU'RE CRAZY: HOW THE
        WORLD'S MOST POWERFUL PSYCHIATRISTS DECIDE
        WHO'S NORMAL (Addison Wesley, 1995)
        Also of note: Figert, Anne E., WOMEN AND THE OWNERSHIP
        OF PMS: THE STRUCTURING OF A PSYCHIATRIC DISORDER
        (Aldine De Gruyter, 1996) ; Herb Kutchins, Herb & Kirk, Stuart A,
        MAKING US CRAZY: DSM: THE PSYCHIATRIC BIBLE AND
        THE CREATION OF MENTAL DISORDERS (Free Press, 1997),
        and Tavris, Carol, THE MISMEASURE OF WOMAN (Simon &
        Schuster, 1992).

53   Kingwell, Mark, BETTER LIVING: IN PURSUIT OF HAPPINESS
        FROM PLATO THE PROZAC, (Penguin books, Toronto, Canada
        1999)

54   http://www.schizophrenia.com/szfacts.htm . Many sources of
        the SUICIDE INCIDENCE FOR PERSONS LIVING WITH

SCHIZOPHRENIA are available for all developed nations. For an excellent listing of evidence-based mental health publications, I recommend The WORLD HEALTH ORGANIZATION. Web Link: http://apps.who.int/bookorders/anglais/catalog_suj1.jsp?sesslan=1&hidsubject=30500

55   Doidge, Dr. Norman, THE BRAIN THAT CHANGES ITSELF: STORIES OF PERSONAL TRIUMPH FROM THE FRONTIERS OF BRAIN SCIENCE, (Penguin Books, New York, NY, 2007)

56   Telfeianb, Albert E., et al, RECOVERY OF LANGUAGE AFTER LEFT HEMISPHERECTOMY IN A SIXTEEN-YEAR-OLD GIRL WITH LATE-ONSET SEIZURES, Pediatric Neurosurgery 2002. Also, see the video about a 6-year girl who had an amazing recovery after a hemispherectomy.: http://alevelpsychology.co.uk/psychology-videos/neuropsychology/brain-plasticity-hemispherectomy.html

57   Underwood, Anne, PROZAC NATION NO MORE, Newsweek, July 8 2008 http://www.newsweek.com/id/144951

58   Frankenburg, R, and Baldessarini, Ross J., NEUROSYPHILIS, MALARIA, AND THE DISCOVERY OF ANTIPSYCHOTIC AGENTS, (Harvard Review of Psychiatry, September 2008)

59   Insel, Dr.Thomas, as quoted by Richard C.Birkel, Director of the NATIONAL INSTITUTE FOR MENTAL HEALTH (NIMH). See report at   http://www.nami.org/

60   Doidge, Dr. Norman, IBID

61   US Food and Drug Administration.   Drug Approvals, Recalls, Consumer and Professional Information on New Discoveries: HTTP://www.fda.gov/

62   Bulletin of the World Health Organization, SMALLPOX AND BIOTERRORISM, Oct 2003

63   Milne, Barry J., Caspi, Avshalom, et al, PREDICTIVE VALUE OF FAMILY HISTORY ON THE SEVERITY OF ILLNESS:

THE CASE FOR DEPRESSION, ANXIETY, ALCOHOL DEPENDENCE, AND DRUG DEPENDENCE, Archives of General Psychiatry. July 2009

64   Schizophrenia.com*. CANNABIS / MARIJUANA (AND OTHER STREET DRUGS) HAVE BEEN LINKED TO SIGNIFICANT INCREASES IN A PERSON'S RISK FOR SCHIZOPHRENIA http://www.schizophrenia.com/prevention/cannabis.marijuana. schizophrenia.html   *leading non-profit organization. Mission: to providing high quality information, support and education to the family members, caregivers and individuals whose lives have been impacted by schizophrenia. Contributors are physicians, researchers and other health care professionals from a large number of universities, worldwide.

65   World Health Organization, MENTAL HEALTH WEBSITE http:// www.who.int/mental_health/en/

66   O'Dea, Frank, WHEN ALL YOU HAVE IS HOPE, Penguin 2007

67   Nuss, Bette, EFT Practitioner, A BETTER WAY TO FEEL, http:// www.eftnow.ca/

68   Dr. Daniel Amen is the mastermind behind programs such as Magnificent Mind at Any Age, and is a frequent program choice on PBS stations.

69   A Level Psychology, GIRL'S LIFE CHANGED AFTER HEMISPHERECTOMY FOR DEBILITATING SEIZURES: video http://alevelpsychology.co.uk/psychology-videos/neuropsychology/ brain-plasticity-hemispherectomy.html

70   Doidge, Dr. Norman, ibid

71   Emile Coué's book, Self-mastery Through Autosuggestion, is now widely available in the public domain, and available in several languages. Though some of what it contains is certainly bizarre, the

basic methods he teaches are similar to those used in therapeutic hypnosis by Psychologists and Psychiatrists today.

72   Moore, Thomas, CARE OF THE SOUL, (New York, NY, 1992)

73   Oz, Dr. Mehmet, Interview. http://oprah.about.com . Better yet, read YOU. THE OWNER'S MANUAL. AN INSIDER'S GUIDE TO THE BODY THAT WILL MAKE YOU HEALTHIER AND YOUNGER, by Dr. Oz, and Dr. Michael F. Roizen

74   Williams, Montel, Interview. www.oprah.com

Chapter 2. Death & Dying

75   Einstein, Albert, Personal Letters (March 1955), as quoted in SCIENCE AND THE SEARCH FOR GOD DISTURBING THE UNIVERSE (1979) by Freeman Dyson, in Chapter 17 "A Distant Mirror"

76   World Health Organization, WORLD HEALTH STATISTICS, 2009

77   Bricker, Darell & Wright, John. Ipsos Reid, WHAT CANADIANS THINK (Random House, Canada, 2005)

78   World Health Organization, WORLD HEALTH REPORT, 2008

79   Cockburn, Bruce, WONDERING WHERE THE LIONS ARE, http://www.cdbaby.com/cd/brucecockburn

80   Kennedy, Charmaine, at DRAGONFLY SEMINAR, 2009, THE TREE OF LIFE NORTH, http://thetreeoflifenorth.com

81   Ovarian Cancer Canada. Cancer de l'Ovaire Canada. http://www.ovariancanada.org/

82   Kubler-Ross, Elizabeth, ON DEATH AND DYING. WHAT THE DYING HAVE TO TEACH DOCTORS AND NURSES CLERGY AND THEIR OWN FAMILY , (Touchstone – Simon & Shuster, New York, 1969)

83   Worden, Dr. J. W., CHILDREN AND GRIEF: WHEN A PARENT DIES, (Guilford Press, New York, NY, 1996)

84   Lok, I.H., &Neugebauer R., PSYCHOLOGICAL MORBIDITY FOLLOWING MISCARRIAGE, (Best Practice & Research, Clinical Obstetrics & Gynecology, April 2007)

85   Cannon, Catherine. GRIEF RECOVERY Specialist. Interview with the author, September 2009. http://www.chcannon.ca/

86   Rachlis, Michael, MD, PRESCRIPTION FOR EXCELLENCE. HOW INNOVATION IS SAVING CANADA'S HEALTH-CARE SYSTEM, (Harper Perennial, Toronto, Canada, 2005). This book is available as a free download at Dr. Rachlis' website http://www.michaelrachlis.com/product.pfe.php

Chapter 3 Catastrophe

87   Trudeau, Pierre Elliot, from the speech delivered in Montréal, February 21, 1971. VIOLENCE, LIBERTY AND QUÉBEC, reprinted in The Readers Digest, July 1971

88   Blanke, Gail, IN MY WILDEST DREAMS, Simon & Schuster, New York, NY 1999). The Carolyn Stradley story is also available on video on her company's website at http://www.cspaving.com/cs_esvideo.html . The interview is from CBS's "The Early Show", with Tracy Smith as the narrator.

89   Orman, Suzy, the "ONE-WOMAN FINANCIAL ADVICE POWERHOUSE." Her website is jam packed with free tools and resources to help you through any financial situation. Http://www.suzeorman.com/

90   Van Dyke, Henry, THE VALLEY OF VISION, (Charles Scribner's Sons. New York, 1920). A gripping, heart-wrenching series of stories and events set in WW1, inspiring and unique.

91   Potts, Malcolm & Haden, Thomas, SEX AND WAR. HOW BIOLOGY EXPLAINS WARFARE AND TERRORISM AND

OFFERS A PATH TO A SAFER WORLD, (Ben Bella Books, 2008)

92   FREE THE CHILDREN, http://www.freethechildren.com/

93   Corbley, Geri Weis, THE GOOD NEWS NETWORK, http://www.goodnewsnetwork.org/

94   Hicks, Esther & Jerry, MONEY AND THE LAW OF ATTRACTION, (Hay House, USA, 2008)

95   IRAN FREES US REPORTER FROM PRISON. http://online.wsj.com/article/SB124204072586206361.html

96   CBC news, PRAYERS, HYMN, HELPED ME SURVIVE ON ICE FLOE, RESCUED SEALER SAYS, (May 7, 2009)

97   Dyer, Dr Wayne, THE POWER OF INTENTION: LEARNING TO CO-CREATE YOUR WORLD YOUR WAY,, (Hay House, Carlsbad, CA, 2004)

98   Wilson, David Sloan, Jerry Lieberman et al, LEARNING FROM MOTHER NATURE ABOUT TEACHING OUR CHILDREN: TEN SIMPLE TRUTHS ABOUT CHILDHOOD EDUCATION FROM AN EVOLUTIONARY PERSPECTIVE. Document published following University of Miami conference

99   CBS News, PRECIOUS: TORONTO FILM FESTIVAL: OSCAR BUZZ BEGINS, Sept 19 2009

100   Benigni, Roberta and cast, LIFE IS BEAUTIFUL (1998) is now available on DVD.

101   St. John Ambulance, http://www.sja.ca/Pages/default.aspx

102   RNRN, REGISTERED NURSE RESPONSE NETWORK, http://www.calnurse.org/rnrn/

103   HEARTS & MINDS, http://www.heartsandminds.org/

Chapter 4. Heartbreak Syndrome

104 Durden,Thomas, HEARTBREAK HOTEL, Much speculation has been written about why Elvis Presley is credited with the writing of this song.

105 Schizophrenia.com, SCHIZOPHRENIA FACTS, http://www.schizophrenia.c om/szfacts.htm . Many sources of suicide incidence for persons living with schizophrenia are available for developed nations. For a reliable GLOBAL LISTING OF EVIDENCE-BASED MENTAL HEALTH PUBLICATIONS, I recommend The World Health Organization. Web Link: http://apps.who.int

106 Seligman, Dr. Martin, AUTHENTIC HAPPINESS, http://www.authentichappiness.sas.upenn.edu/Default.aspx

107 THE SEDONA METHOD, http://www.sedona.com/

108 www.womens-law-of-attraction-solutions.com

Chapter 5. Workplace Challenges

109 VisionarEase Inc., TURNING CRISIS INTO OPPORTUNITY© is a copyrighted workshop, all rights reserved.

110 Bolles, Dick, WHAT COLOR IS YOUR PARACHUTE? (Berkeley, California, 2009). Long considered the gold standard for re-creating your work life.

111 Gerard Seijts, Gerard, quoted in "NIX THE CHEERFEST IF PEOPLE HAVE BEEN LAID OFF." The Globe and Mail, Monday, March 16, 2009

112 Landes, David L., THE WEALTH AND POVERTY OF NATIONS. Why some are so rich and some so poor, (W. W. Norton & Co., New York, NY, 2009)

113 Cooperrider, David and Whitney, Diana, APPRECIATIVE INQUIRY. A POSITIVE REVOLUTION IN CHANGE (San Francisco, California, 2005).

Suggested website: Appreciative Inquiry Commons www. appreciativeinquiry.ckkkase.edu

114 Lee, Isabella, TOP NOTCH TAX PROFESSIONAL EMBRACES CARING CULTURE, Career Times, March 7, 2008. Full article available as PDF: http://ia310825.us.archive.org

115 Senge, Peter, THE FIFTH DISCIPLINE. THE ART AND PRACTICE OF THE LEARNING ORGANIZATION (Doubleday, New York, NY, 1994)

116 Sharma, Robin, LEADERSHIP WISDOM FROM THE MONK WHO SOLD HIS FERRARI. THE 8 RITUALS OF VISIONARY LEADERS, (Harper Collins, Publishers Ltd., Toronto Ontario Canada, 1998)

117 Stanley, Bessie Anderson, SUCCESS, 1904.

Chapter 6. Caregiver Burnout

118 Baroness Pitkeathley is currently the chairwoman of the New Opportunities Fund, UK

119 Health and Human Services. INFORMAL CAREGIVING: COMPASSION IN ACTION. Washington, DC: Department of Health and Human Services. Based on data from the National Survey of Families and Households (NSFH), 1998.

120 Caregivers. Backgrounder. UNPAID CAREGIVING IN CANADA. http://www.hrsdc.gc.ca/eng/cs/comm/sd/caregivers.shtml

121 World Wide Home Care Statistics, TRENDS AND THE FOUR PILLAR SOLUTION TO CAREGIVER/CARER CHALLENGES. This is an excellent template for change in the sector and to help people experiencing caregiver burnout. Now available on PDF at http://www.womenrisingnow.com

122 Ibid

123   Rogers, Ann, WOMEN ARE HERE TO STAY, Harper's Magazine, (November, 1952)

124   Chappell, Neena, as quoted by John Lorinc in FAMILY VALUE, Zoomer magazine, September 2009

Chapter 7. Health & Wellness

125   Weil, Dr. Andrew, 4-7-8 BREATHING is based on Dr. Weil's expert techniques. http://www.drweil.com/

126   Al Sharar, Dr. Ben, HAPPINESS 101, PBS, September 2009

127   HEART & STROKE. A few help web sites. Canada: http://ww2.heartandstroke.ca/splash/ , US http://www.hearthub.org/ , UK http://www.bhf.org.uk/ , Africa http://www.comminit.com/en/node/266097/38 , Australia http://www.healthinsite.gov.au/topics/Heart__Stroke_and_Vascular_Health , The Americas http://www.circ.ahajournals.org/cgi/content/full/95/10/2335/a

128   CANCER. A few help web sites. Canada http://www.cancer.ca/?sc_lang=en , US http://www.cancer.org/docroot/home/index.asp , UK http://www.cancerindex.org/clink44k.htm , Africa http://www.cansa.org.za/cgi-bin/giga.cgi?c=1056 , Australia http://www.cancer.org.au/Home.htm , South America http://www.sbcancer.org.br/

129   Halle Berry http://www.diabetesaware.com/

130   Roizen, Michael F., Oz, Mehmet C., YOU THE OWNER'S MANUAL, (Harper Collins, New York, NY, 2005)

131   POSITIVE RELAXATION 101: http://www.cdbaby.com/cd/giseleguenard

132   American Journal of Cardiology, LIVE LONGER WITH MEDITATION, 2005, http://www.ajconline.org/

133   Kristoff, Prof, Kalina, Press Release in Science Daily's BRAIN'S PROBLEM SOLVING FUNCTION AT WORK WHEN

WE DAYDREAM, May 2009, http://www.sciencedaily.com/releases/2009/05/090511180702.htm

134   Goldman, Dr. Brian, WHITE COAT BLACK ART. http://www.cbc.ca/whitecoat/2009/08/burnout_try_looking_in_the_mir.html

135   McGraw, Phil, http://www.drphil.com , also see SELF MATTERS: CREATING YOUR LIFE FROM THE INSIDE OUT, (Simon & Suster, New York, NY, 2001)

136   LOOK GOOD FEEL BETTER, Canadian survey of impact: https://www.lgfb.ca/uploads/assets//Press_Releases/U.S._Survey_Press_Release.pdf

137   BBC News, April 2008, MAN GROWS END OF FINGER BACK http://news.bbc.co.uk/2/hi/health/7354458.stm

138   LiveStrong, Lance Armstrong Foundation, http://www.livestrong.org/site/c.khLXK1PxHmF/b.2660611/k.BCED/Home.htm

139   Duke, Patty, PATTY DUKE ONLINE CENTER FOR MENTAL WELLNESS, http://www.pattyduke.net

140   Independent Panel for Special Education Advice DAVINA: A TRIBUTE, http://www.ipsea.org.uk/davina-tribute.htm

141   National MS Society, Annette Funicello, http://www.nationalmssociety.org/online-community/personal-stories/annette-funicello/index.aspx

142   Levy BR, et al. LONGEVITY INCREASED BY POSITIVE SELF-PERCEPTIONS OF AGING. (Journal of Personality and Social Psychology. 2002 Aug)

CPSIA information can be obtained at www.ICGtesting.com
Printed in the USA
237788LV00001B/205/P